"At the center of human commu[...] holidays, family gatherings, part[...] only to the fulfillment of our phy[...] for God and each other which so[...] many feasts of Scripture, Alicia does a wonderful job connecting us to this sacred longing of ours. After reading this book, it will be difficult for you to think of any meal as insignificant again."

Scott Sauls, senior pastor of Christ Presbyterian Church and author
of *A Gentle Answer* and *Beautiful People Don't Just Happen*

"Who doesn't love a great meal—the best of ingredients, prepared by an excellent cook, and presented in a way that awakens our appetite? That's what *Invitations to Abundance* is. It is rich food for heart, mind, and soul—filled with the best of ingredients, the Scripture, and prepared by a creative and insightful writer who presents the truths of Scripture and the beauty of Christ in a way that makes us hungry for more of him."

Nancy Guthrie, author and Bible teacher

"Jesus' promise of abundant life has become for some a hope for more stuff, better health, or a shortcut to fame. Alicia Akins' beautiful, faithful writing offers readers powerful reorientation toward the kind of abundance to which Jesus refers as she traces the themes of feasting through Scripture. The hospitality God offers—his invitation to remember and experience for ourselves his gifts of deliverance, mercy, wisdom, and more—will reorient us toward true abundance as we find our places at his table."

Michelle Van Loon, author of *Moments and Days:
How Our Holy Celebrations Shape Our Faith*

"This book is a banquet, a ten-course meal celebrating who God is, what God has done, and who God is calling us to be. Akins invites us to the table to rest in God's love, feast on God's goodness, and be refreshed by God's Spirit. A stunning, faithful, poetic debut."

Courtney Ellis, author of *Uncluttered* and *Happy Now*

"In this much-needed reflection on the significance of feasting in scripture and in our shared lives together, Alicia J. Akins has spread for readers her own nurturing and savory feast of hope, healing, remembrance, celebration, expectation, and longing. Who among us does not ache to be present at that final wedding feast toward which all of history is flowing, in a day when all our losses are restored and sufferings redeemed? Alicia's thoughtful essays fan the flames of that same eternal ache, even while offering us a more rooted sense of our own place in the long history of redemption. I will continue to ponder the themes of this book for years to come."

Douglas Kaine McKelvey, author of *Every Moment Holy*

"In *Invitations to Abundance*, Alicia pulls together the many feasts introduced throughout Scripture, probing their depth to understand what they reveal about one another and the nature of God. From the Israelites' mandated feasts to the imagery of feasts in the wisdom literature and the life and parables of Jesus, the book looks ahead to the culmination of all feasts in the promised feast to come: the Marriage Supper of the Lamb. This book is for all who love to taste and see God's goodness in the words of Scripture."

Kendall Vanderslice, author of *We Will Feast: Rethinking Dinner, Worship, and the Community of God*

"The hardships of life in this world have the ability distort our view of God into as a stingy, closed-fisted master. In *Invitations to Abundance,* Alicia Akins beautifully portrays for us God's actual delight in being a Lord who lavishly provides. Through the pages of the book and the rhythm of liturgy, she welcomes us to the feast. Come, eat, and be filled."

Rev. Dr. Irwyn L. Ince, Jr., author of *The Beautiful Community*

"Alicia Akins' book is a beautiful work of practical theology—a delicious, filling meal. Weaving her way expertly through the feasts of the Bible, Akins helps us see God as humanity's consummate host. Then, discovering our place as guests at his table, we learn to give thanks, practice dependence, and persevere in suffering. This is the kind of book that both nourishes and leaves you hungry—to taste and see for yourself that the Lord is good."

Jen Pollock Michel, award-winning author of *Surprised by Paradox* and *A Habit Called Faith*

"Through her book, *Invitations to Abundance*, Alicia Akins invites us into a rhythm of remembering, delighting, and experiencing God through the practice of feasting in the Bible. She hosts us at the table, explaining the context and reasons for the feasts and teaching us their meaning for our faith today. Each chapter ends with a liturgy—a needed pause and reflection, like a satisfied sigh at the end of a delicious meal. Receive God's invitation to come and eat through this book, and your soul will be fed."

Grace P. Cho, writer, poet, and speaker

Invitations to ABUNDANCE

ALICIA J. AKINS

HARVEST HOUSE PUBLISHERS
EUGENE, OREGON

Bible translations quoted in this book can be found at end of the book.

Cover designed by Studio Gearbox, Chris Gilbert

Interior design by Angie Renich, Wildwood Digital Publishing

Cover photo © Oksana.Bondar / Shutterstock

For bulk, special sales, or ministry purchases, please call 1-800-547-8979. Email: Customerservice@hhpbooks.com

This logo is a federally registered trademark of the Hawkins Children's LLC. Harvest House Publishers, Inc., is the exclusive licensee of this trademark.

Invitations to Abundance
Copyright © 2022 by Alicia J. Akins
Published by Harvest House Publishers
Eugene, Oregon 97408
www.harvesthousepublishers.com

ISBN 978-0-7369-8427-0 (pbk)
ISBN 978-0-7369-8428-7 (eBook)

LCCN: 2021937785

Printed in the United States of America
22 23 24 25 26 27 28 29 30 / BP / 10 9 8 7 6 5 4 3 2 1

Contents

INTRODUCTION

You hold in your hands an invitation to a feast. Or more accurately, twelve of them. They are invitations I myself have received, sometimes accepting them, other times sending regrets.

Each chapter of *Invitations to Abundance* begins with the addressee, then goes on to explain the occasion: what's being offered, who's in attendance, and what to expect at the table. It situates you in the room. Closing each chapter is an RSVP in the form of a liturgical response. These short pieces provide you with suggested ways to say, "Yes, I will be in attendance." My hope is that they could be incorporated into your regular rhythms of prayer as needed.

The Bible turns regularly to the imagery of a feast. By taking a closer look at these themes we can better understand how God wants to be approached and experienced. So the invitations to feast contained here are drawn from every major section of the Bible. We begin with the feasts that God mandated for the people of Israel. Then we look at feasting in wisdom literature and poetry. From there we move to the prophets and historical books before turning to the New Testament. Two chapters feature feasts from parables found in the Gospels. Then, finally, we look at the Lord's Supper and the Wedding Supper of the Lamb.

When I lived in Laos, I was once invited to a Lao coworker's home to celebrate the New Year. He and his family had prepared quite the spread for me. Whenever my eating slowed or my plate neared being clear, I was offered more. After eating more than I even knew possible, I laid out on the floor, unable to move. Then a knock came at the door. The neighbors also wanted to feed me. I managed to pull myself off the floor to venture next door and out came another huge pile of food, except this time the entire pile was for me. I didn't know what to do. I could not put one more bite of food in my mouth, and here I was presented with food enough for a small family.

I often think about this experience when I think about what God has for me—and for you. What if God gave us feasts so we could understand him better? What if these meals that seem to be universal point not just to the eternal, but to a table set every day that awaits us? What if we lived like that were true?

These were the questions that birthed this book. After a long season of hardship where I felt glued to God's table, I wanted to explore the idea more. By all measures during that time my life was far from what most would call prosperous, and yet I felt so full. Into my weariness came a knock at the door followed by dish after dish of God's goodness. My hope for you as you read is that you too would find yourself at God's table, partaking of all the goodness he has for you.

Chapter 1

DELIVERANCE REMEMBERED

To the Captive

Blessed are You, Our God, Sovereign of the universe, who has chosen us from among the peoples, exalting us by hallowing us with mitzvot.[1] In Your love, Adonai our God, You have given us feasts of gladness, and seasons of joy; this Festival of Pesach,[2] season of our freedom, a sacred occasion, a remembrance of the Exodus from Egypt. For You have chosen us from all peoples and consecrated us to Your service, and given us the Festivals, a time of gladness and joy.

KIDDUSH, A JEWISH BLESSING TO START THE PASSOVER SEDER

Fear of being unseen, unheard, and ultimately unrescued tyrannized the souls of God's people. *Does God see us? Can he hear us? Will he save?* But Israel had yet to plumb the full depths of its own slavery: While Egyptian slave masters exploited their bodies, their short memories, scarcity mindset, and nearsightedness exploited their minds. Whatever deliverance God planned for his people needed to defeat both enemies. So came the first of many Lord-ordained feasts, the Passover, where God connected desperate need to divine supply. Through this feast and its memorial, God would overwrite the effects of sin on his people's memory, mindset, vision, and identity.

Like a spotlight to a stage, the full Egyptian moon shone down on the land as the theater of redemption drew back the curtains on its next act. On the eve of a spectacular rescue, a few precious splatters of blood had determined which parents hugged their firstborns tight, releasing into the night long, unwittingly held breaths, and which parents cradled limp bodies, piercing the darkness with the anguished wails of child loss.

Pharaoh summoned Moses.

Earlier that evening, after another grueling day of labor, the Israelites had returned to their homes to prepare the special meal the Lord commanded. Calloused hands rolled unleavened dough for *matzah*. Already fatigued arms slaughtered unblemished, year-old lambs at twilight, careful not to break any bones. One family member dipped the purple-plumed ends of hyssop twigs in the lamb's blood to brush it on the doorposts and lintel of their home. Another readied a fire to roast the lamb.

Entire households sat—belts fastened, sandals on, and staves in hand—devouring the lamb, unleavened bread, and bitter herbs. All was to be eaten before midnight. What remained at dawn would be burned. Predictions swirled about what the morning would bring.

"Up, go out from among my people, both you and the people of Israel," Pharaoh conceded, reversing his prior rejection of Moses' requests. "Go, serve the LORD, as you have said. Take your flocks and your herds, as you have said, and be gone" (Exodus 12:31-32). Once word of this midnight meeting made it back to the Israelites, they were as eager to leave as the Egyptians were to see them go. In their rush to escape, the Israelites grabbed unleavened dough, kneading bowls, and silver and gold jewelry and clothes they'd acquired earlier from the Egyptians. They set out, their firstborn sons in tow—reminders of God's protection. After a short journey, they arrived—free men, women, and children—at the bank of the sea.

Betrayed. Disillusioned. Resigned to return to their slavery. Wedged between untamable sea and approaching enemy chariots, their minds flooded with doubts. Sure, they avoided war with the Philistines by taking a longer, less direct path—one divinely guided by pillars of cloud and fire. But that path dead-ended at the sea. What sick twist had them lose to the sea after all they'd survived? To end up cornered by their old oppressor with no exit in sight meant Egypt had outmaneuvered the great I AM. Wouldn't it have been better to serve the Egyptians than to die by their hand in the desert? But God could not be cornered. Though Israel couldn't see it, God saw the far side of the sea, and freedom for them was still on his horizon. His way went through the depths.

At God's rebuke, the sea dried as the waters rushed into place like soldiers snapping to attention. To Israel's rear, God dispatched darkness to block the Egyptians' way so Israel could advance unseen. As they crossed the sea by faith, no sloshing of sandals could be heard, no mud clung to their heels. Instead, they crossed, as through a desert, kicking up seafloor dust with each step. After Israel's safe passage, the same sea that aided Israel swallowed the Egyptian chariots and horsemen whole.

Stunned, from the distant shore Israel looked back in awe and relief. At long last, freedom! Not by revolt nor by self-determination, but by the strong hand and outstretched arm of God they stood redeemed. Slavery was behind them and could reach no further.

The entire camp broke into song:

> I will sing to the LORD, for he has triumphed gloriously;
> the horse and the rider he has thrown into the sea (Exodus 15:1).

LIBERTY TO CAPTIVES

Passover both *is* this story and tells this story. You could fit all this on a plate, and they did. The tastes and textures of the meal captured and retold the details of Israel's deliverance. The smokiness of the roasted lamb, each grain of flour for *matzah*, and the bite of bitter herbs recalled Israel's 400-plus years' bondage and their release.

Even their eating posture made a statement. They ate the first Passover seated, while the memorial meal was eaten reclining, the posture of the free.[3] All participants in the feast, regardless of status or station, ate in this manner. At this meal, the blood made them all equals.

Israel had been living as foreigners in Egypt for over four hundred years, and for most of it, they'd been viewed as a threat and enslaved. Exodus 1:12-14 describes the dynamic between Egypt and Israel:

> The Egyptians were in dread of the people of Israel. So
> they ruthlessly made the people of Israel work as slaves
> and made their lives bitter with hard service, in mortar
> and brick and in all kinds of work in the field. In all their
> work they ruthlessly made them work as slaves.

Egypt was merciless and Israel was buckling under the strain.

Behind the scenes, God had long been preparing for Israel's deliverance, as evidenced by Moses surviving Pharaoh's infanticide campaign and then being adopted by the Pharaoh's daughter. God had not for one moment been unaware of what his people were suffering, even if it was not obvious to them he was doing much at all. Exodus 2:23-24 says, "Their cry for rescue from slavery came up to God. And God heard their groaning, and God remembered his covenant with Abraham, with Isaac, and with Jacob." God saw the people of Israel—and God knew. He had seen. He could hear. He would save. Soon he would take the stage.

As God sent Moses on his way, he instructed him to tell Pharaoh Israel was his son, "You shall say to Pharaoh, 'Thus says the LORD, Israel is my firstborn son'" (Exodus 4:22). God was claiming Israel not just as a nation, but, for the first time, as his child. He would care for them accordingly. James Bruckner writes, "For the first time here, scripture portrays God as *a parent defending their child.*"[4]

What parent does not keep watch over their child? Or does not hear their cries and try to discern what they need? And what parent, knowing what their child needs, does not rush to give it to them? The timing wasn't insignificant either: this parent-child relationship was rooted in God's deliverance. As Irish biblical scholar J.A. Motyer puts it, "It was there that sonship and salvation were indissolubly linked."[5] God was a parent who rescued.

God sent Moses to negotiate for relief for Israel. But as soon as Moses made the request, Egyptian taskmasters multiplied their workload, forcing them to meet their daily quota for brick-making despite no longer giving them the needed straw. The harsher conditions were meant to preoccupy the Israelites so they couldn't give second thought to their release. Many weary Israelites started to think freedom was more trouble than it was worth, and Moses could not shake them from their despondency. Though he reminded them of God's grand intentions toward them, Exodus 6:9 says, "They did not listen to Moses because of their broken spirit and harsh slavery." Despite Moses' efforts, they'd lost hope their lives could get better and simply prayed they wouldn't get worse.

A Plague Like No Other

Nine times, Moses made his appeal to Pharaoh. Nine times, a refusal and plagues followed. Passover, the tenth and final plague God sent to get Pharaoh to comply, stood out from the rest in several ways. First, it was the ultimate faceoff between God and the deities of Egypt. Each prior plague dealt with one of Egypt's many gods. The tenth plague, however, executed judgment on all the gods of Egypt at once, showcasing God's sovereignty over them all.

Moses also foretold the last plague from the beginning. Before any of the other plagues had happened, God instructed Moses to tell Pharaoh this would all end with the death of Egyptian firstborns (Exodus 4:23). Pharaoh had ample warning, the escalation was due to his hardness of heart.

Further, with all but the plague of the gnats, it was clear Egypt alone would suffer while Israel would not. Israel was exempt from the others automatically. With the tenth plague, however, individual cooperation was required. They had to select a lamb, house it for three days, slaughter it without breaking any of its bones, and put its blood on their doors. *Then* when God saw the blood, he would spare them from death. The blood alone, and not God's special affection for his people, would keep death from Israel's door. As Motyer puts it, "Previously they had been segregated by the Lord without any cooperative or obedient act of their own, but now by command of the Lord, Israel must take a stand, self-declared as the people under the blood of the lamb."[6] When it came to the blood of the lamb, Israel could not be passive.

The death of the firstborn sons was also unique in that while either Moses or Aaron had played roles in the other plagues, here God acts alone, and on an astounding scale. Unlike other plagues, the death of firstborns was singularly effected by God himself entering Egypt.

PASSOVER INSTITUTED

The Passover was the first memorial day—*zikkaron* in Hebrew—of its kind in the Bible. Passover was the first annual reminder God set for his people, the first day set apart for them. Even before they were told to keep the Sabbath, they were told to keep the Passover. And God was adamant: the Passover was to be a "statute forever," "throughout your generations" (Exodus 12:14, 17). Even after they entered Canaan, it was to continue: "When you come to the land that the LORD will give you as he has promised, you shall keep this service" (Exodus 12:25). God even required that they travel to Jerusalem to celebrate together (Deuteronomy 16:16). This day commemorated God seeing the blood of the paschal lamb on the Israelites' doors and sparing their firstborn sons. An extravagant act in its own right, Passover also served as the prelude to an escape no one but God could have imagined.

The Passover was not just momentous for Israel but was defining for God as well. He would go from being known as the God of Abraham, Isaac, and Jacob, as he'd first introduced himself to Moses (Exodus 3:6), to being known as the Lord who brought Israel out of Egypt. There was a brand shift about to take place from God being the God of the patriarchs to God being redeemer of a nation.

"Passover" describes the historical event and its commemorative observances. The first Passover was on the fourteenth day of the first month of the Jewish calendar. The Feast of Unleavened Bread then starts the following day and continues for seven days to the twenty-first. On the first and last of these days, no work was permitted. Originally, these festivals were separate, but by late antiquity,[7] they'd merged into one. Today, Passover often refers to both festivals, from the fourteenth to the twenty-first. I will refer to the first night as Passover and the following nights as the Feast of Unleavened Bread.

FEAST OF UNLEAVENED BREAD

The Feast of Unleavened Bread harkened back to a hasty exit. This seven-day festival reminded Israel not just of their quick departure, but also of the strong hand of the Lord in clearing a way through the sea.

For seven days they were to eat nothing with leaven. A thorough spring cleaning ensured not even the crumbs of anything that had undergone the leavening process, by any agent, remained in any homes. But not only that, no leaven was to be found in their entire territory. The penalty for not removing the yeast from their homes was to be cut off from their community. It was not enough to be free of Egypt;

worship and unleavening must follow. It might seem strange to base a feast on what you *can't* eat, but both Passover and the Feast of Unleavened Bread were about so much more.

CULINARY TIME TRAVEL

The concept of culinary time travel is not as foreign as we might think. The other day, I traveled by mouth back to Laos, a Southeast Asian country where I used to live. After procuring all the ingredients I needed to make one of my favorite Lao dishes, I set them all out on the counter and got to work opening bottles, measuring, mixing. Even before the first taste, I had escaped through scent and texture to a different time and place. Just one whiff and my favorite sauce sent me back to the sun-soaked streets of Luang Prabang. I laughed as I reopened the bottle a second and third time and transported somewhere different with each smell. I was standing in my kitchen but also standing before the lunch stall where I was a regular, exploring the night market, and al fresco dining riverside with friends. The food had facilitated a return to time past.

The link between food and memory is strong. In *The Omnivorous Mind,* neuroscientist John S. Allen writes,

> Food memories are important not just because they concern sustenance but also because they have extensive connections to other memories of people, places, and things...In humans, the complex associations and flexible expressions of these kinds of memories, combined with our well-developed executive functions, contribute to our unprecedented ability to turn previous experiences into future plans and actions...Many of our food memories can be classified as autobiographical memories concerning food.[8]

This was the point of observing the Passover. The *Pesachim,* a Jewish manual on how to celebrate the Passover, states, "In every generation a man is obligated to regard himself as though he personally had gone forth from Egypt."[9] Even by the second recorded observance of Passover upon settling in Canaan, no eyewitness to the Egyptian exodus survived. Before you think it far-fetched for a nation to memorialize events no living person had experienced, remember that our own holidays commemorate national victories outside living memory. For Israel, the Lord chose food to help mediate that experience. Revisiting their past through food could strengthen their faith as they faced fresh trials.

The Passover was not, and is not, concerned with the volume of food, but with what the table evokes. It transports God's people back to their slavery in Egypt so they can relive that paradigm-crushing deliverance through curated food and ritual. The evening's flavors reconstitute forgotten details of their autobiography, propelling Israel toward futures aligned with who they are and, more importantly, toward God's grander story. Philosopher Alasdair MacIntyre recognized we live as people of our story, writing: "But the key question for men is not about their own authorship; I can only answer the question 'What am I to do?' if I can answer the prior question 'Of what story or stories do I find myself a part?'"[10] The table affirmed that their story's hero held both the heart of the king and the depths of the sea in his hands and could enact miraculous deliverance.

The Passover was like an old photo album in culinary form. They were eating their story, and as they did, it nourished them. There weren't heaps of food, but there didn't need to be. The right foods— the lamb, the unleavened bread, and bitter herbs—would tell the story they'd do well to remember. Like a doctor prescribing medicine, God insists on the Passover for Israel's good. Their need to remember would only grow the further from the exodus they got. If not careful, what remained after generations of neglecting their story would be nothing more than tepid trust in a fast-shrinking God.

THE PASSOVER LAMB

Israel owed their lives to the lamb. In Exodus 4:22, God pronounced all of Israel his firstborn, and yet firstborns were the very target of his Passover judgment. Blood of the lamb withstanding, Israel would not have survived the night. The lamb at the Passover memorial meal reminded them of the protection offered in its blood, but the preparation of its body held meaning as well. The lamb could only be roasted and could not be cooked using any other method, harkening back to the idea of haste permeating the entire meal. Roasting was the way to cook when you packed light, as if you had left in a hurry, as they did. It was the cooking method associated with travel.[11] While it wasn't the quickest way to cook the lamb, it required the least equipment and, considering the lamb's sacredness, also provided the least chance for cross-contamination. The lamb not only allowed them to avoid bloodshed that evening but precipitated their emancipation and hasty escape.

The Passover lamb was carefully chosen for condition and size. Those presenting offerings knew to bring only the unblemished before God, as ritual instructions specified animal sacrifices must be blemish-free and without defect. The lamb was also chosen based on size and the number of people who were going to eat it. The command was: "According to what each can eat you shall make your count for the lamb" (Exodus 12:4). Households of fewer than ten and individuals without relatives joined with larger families so they were not burdened with eating the entire animal on their own, since none was supposed to be left past midnight.[12] Those who had enough to spare were to be mindful of the more isolated within their community; deliverance for all was incompatible with "every man for himself." The most suitable lamb for the meal wasn't just one without blemish to satisfy God's judgment, but one that had been selected by taking into account the exact needs of those at every table. The lamb met both God's need and the people's.

Unleavened Bread

Before the Passover and Feast of Unleavened Bread began, God's people rid their homes of all leaven, down to the smallest breadcrumb. Prohibited food items included wheat, oats, spelt, and rye. Barley was included if it had been exposed to water for longer than 18 minutes, after which point it underwent a kind of leavening.[13] Beer and wine, due to the fermentation process, also could not remain. Not only was leaven forbidden from their homes, it was not to be found anywhere nearby. The whole land needed to be purged.

The leavening process and leaven came to be used in the Bible symbolically, becoming associated in Israel's imagination with life under slavery. Though invisible, a small amount could pervade an entire substance. Only rarely is this spoken of as a boon. More often than not, it was seen as harmful to spiritual progress and maturity. For instance, Jesus warned his listeners about the Pharisees and Sadducees, likening their teaching to leaven (Matthew 16:6; Mark 8:15; Luke 12:1). And in 1 Corinthians, Paul tells the church to be on alert for leaven, calling them unleavened people of sincerity and truth (1 Corinthians 5:6-8).

Bitter Herbs

The Passover table held not only lamb and unleavened bread, but also bitter herbs—often lettuce or chicory. These represented the harsh conditions Israel left behind. Why not just eat lamb to remember being spared, or the bread to remember their hasty escape? Why remember their misery too? The lamb was tied to the bitter herbs, as their salvation was tied to the bitter cruelty from which they'd been released. This juxtaposition sweetened the rescue.

For a long time, in my naivete, I thought, *How kind of Christ to die for me.* Not being able to grasp my sinfulness, I had no way to appraise the true worth of his sacrifice. Only when I began to see myself as sinful, and incorrigibly so, did his sacrifice become incalculable to me. My salvation began to mean something more than a ticket to heaven; it represented a break from a ruthless past. Not until I see my slavery for what it was, in all its bitterness, can I see my deliverance from it for what it is. The deeper my understanding of my slavery, the more precious to me my rescue. Seeing the lamb and bread and bitter herbs in proper relation to each other adds weight and meaning to salvation and deliverance.

Among foods recalling hardship, the bitter herbs had company on the table. Another dish included in Jewish Passover celebrations today is charoset, a mix of fruit and nuts. It symbolizes the brick and mortar used in their hard labor. We can carry a vague sense of our slavery, but the more specific we can be about the ways we've been enslaved, the more particular our understanding, and the more precious the lamb.

EGYPT MISREMEMBERED

When slavery starts to look appealing again and we no longer even recognize it for what it is, we can know we've forgotten the Lord. Do old sin patterns seem more appealing than harmful? Would I rather work for the approval of others than be freed by the love and acceptance of God? Am I content to live as though the only power I have available to me is my own? Do I keep myself from joy by defaulting to comparison? Have I begun to think of God as a consolation prize rather than as my very great reward? In Deuteronomy 6:12, Moses warned the people of Israel, "Take care lest you forget the Lord, who brought you out of the land of Egypt, out of the house of slavery." Yet Israel did not observe the Passover in the wilderness. Instead, as they wandered, they clung to a distorted sense of nostalgia for the land they'd left behind. They chronically misremembered the heavy yoke of oppression and looked back on their slavery with fondness. They reminisced about their varied diet in Egypt of fish that cost nothing, cucumbers, melons, leeks, onions, and garlic, but complained about the abundance of manna and "worthless food" God provided (Numbers 21:5). And when they found Meribah waterless, they grumbled again.

They grew unruly after the spies' report about the promised land and its intimidating inhabitants, and they longed for the "good old days" of Egypt. This cost an entire generation the chance to enter the promised land. Eventually, they drifted so far from Passover truth that they even accused God of hating them and being cruel for delivering them at all. The Israelites were starved for their story.

Their inability to correctly remember Egypt and the Passover would also hinder them from keeping other commands. Several times, God instructs Israel and then adds that they are to obey because of what happened in Egypt. Their ability to live fearless, generous, and just lives counted on it. For example, they were commanded not to fear other nations because they remembered what God did to Pharaoh (Exodus 7:1-5). The Sabbatical year, in which debts were canceled and servants freed with generous gifts of grain and wine, was also rooted in Passover remembrance: "As the Lord your God has blessed you, you shall give to him. You shall remember that you were a slave in the land of Egypt, and the Lord your God redeemed you; therefore I command you this today" (Deuteronomy 15:14-15). And God again appealed to their memory when he told them to give the sojourner, fatherless, and widow their due justice: "Remember that you were a slave in Egypt and the Lord your God redeemed you from there; therefore I command you to do this" (Deuteronomy 24:18).

The potency and accuracy of Israel's memory of Egypt would influence not just how they saw God and themselves but their disadvantaged and vulnerable neighbors. Israel's acts of generosity, justice, and mercy were inextricably tied to the rescue they themselves had experienced.

A FEAST TO REMEMBER

At the Red Sea, God provided Israel with more than just an exit.

He'd storied them with a God so mighty yet attentive that the next challenge should've seemed small by comparison. The Passover was the Romans 8:32 of its day. "He who did not spare his own Son but gave him up for us all, how will he not also with him graciously give us all things?" If God had performed the most grandiose, how could they not also trust him with the most granular? If the chaos of the sea could be subdued to allow them safe passage, what couldn't God do?

This is true for us too. Our Father did the most grandiose so we'd trust him with the most granular. Like Israel, we too were spared by the blood of our Passover lamb. Like them, we were rescued with a deliverance powerful enough to overwrite our broken memory, mind, vision, and identity. Our redemption retrofitted our thinking for the unfathomable, corrected our vision for the greater story, and rooted our identity in being rescued children of the Most High. Freed of fruitless toil and oppression, we now go after the leaven in our lives and communities. Theologian Philip Ryken writes, "The Feast of Unleavened Bread reminds us of what God wants us to do once we've been saved, and that is to live a sanctified life, becoming more and more freed from sin."[14] We keep watch for those sins that are harder to observe, that can be baked into good works, or that are culturally acceptable: unforgiveness, selfishness, fierce independence, unresolved conflict, pride, materialism, to name a few. These things often hinder our growth without our even knowing it.

Just as we, like Israel, have been freed, we too need to cultivate a practice of remembrance. It is right and good to pause on occasions—Easter, Communion—to recall the severity, beauty, and mercy of the cross. But annual and weekly reminders are not enough when sin and doubt crouch daily at our door. God knew Israel would need to jog their own memory, and we need to jog ours as well. What good are all the incredible and mighty works of the Lord on our behalf if we live as though they never happened? God does not desire a kingdom of amnesiacs, but of long-memoried people.

One of my favorites ways to do this is through what I call a goodness inventory—a sort of highlight reel of faithfulness, where I reflect on God's faithfulness beginning each sentence with "Did he not...?" I usually begin by reading Psalm 78. Then, starting from Genesis and working my way through the Bible, I try to recall as many mighty acts God performed on behalf of his people as I can. When I run out of examples from the Bible, I turn to personal stories from my life of God's faithfulness. Finally, I turn to the testimonies of friends. I try to exhaust every example in my memory. I've found it powerful to then revisit my present doubt, this time against the backdrop of the examples of God's faithfulness. I use this practice most often when I'm staring down despair and hopelessness. Even though I don't do it daily, the cumulative effect of reciting such an exhaustive list lingers for a while and encourages easier recall over time.

A daily practice I've turned to in the past has been to change my morning alarm to a song that reminds me of God's faithfulness and to let it play for a while in the morning as I wake rather than rushing to turn it off. The day greets me with a reminder of God's goodness. I also often write about times God has brought me through difficulties and then go back and reread what I've written when I next struggle to believe God sees or cares for me.

But I also try to cultivate relationships where it's routine to share about where we see God at work, in our own lives and in one another's lives. My housemate and I have been praying together every Tuesday morning for several years now, and every so often I'll print out a list of past requests and see how they've been answered. This was a practice I also did with my former small group. Before we went on break for the summer, I'd print out each person's requests on one side of a sheet of paper, leaving the other side blank for everyone to record how God answered them. After a time of personal reflection, we'd each share with the group how God had answered our prayers over the past year. Some of these examples found their way into my goodness inventory.

What, after all, are we to remember? The constantly moving goalposts for success that wearied us? The futile and unrelenting search for significance and belonging that perplexed us? The self-help Band-Aid we put over our insecurities that disappointed us? Or plagues that passed us over and paths that appeared where we expected dead ends? We remember it all—the taxing and the liberating. Our labor was backbreaking, but then came the lamb. We remember its blood covered us. We remember it freed us to worship. God broke our bondage to sin; it is no longer our master. We also remember we are the firstborn son of a father who sees, hears, and saves. God is supreme not only over the pantheon of Egyptian deities but over the local deities of our lives as well. But first, we remember God wants us to remember, and that if these truths are to do us or our neighbor any good, we must deliberately remember deliverance as a statute, throughout all generations and every one of our days.

> When your son asks you in time to come, "What is the meaning of the testimonies and the statutes and the rules that the Lord our God has commanded you?" then you shall say to your son, "We were Pharaoh's slaves in Egypt. And the Lord brought us out of Egypt with a mighty hand. And the Lord showed signs and wonders, great and grievous, against Egypt and against Pharaoh and all his household, before our eyes. And he brought us out from there, that he might bring us in and give us the land that he swore to give to our fathers. And the Lord commanded us to do all these statutes, to fear the Lord our God, for our good always, that he might preserve us alive, as we are this day. And it will be righteousness for us, if we are careful to do all this commandment before the Lord our God, as he has commanded us."
> —Deuteronomy 6:20-25

LITURGY FOR REMEMBRANCE

You have led in your steadfast love the
people whom you have redeemed;
You have guided them by your strength to your holy abode.

Exodus 15:13

I am the Lord your God, who brought
you up out of the land of Egypt.
Open your mouth wide, and I will fill it.

Psalm 81:10

Almighty Deliverer and Sovereign,
God who sees and hears and saves:
spared from death and seafared to freedom,
I trust and delight in you.

Keep your servant from trying to repatriate to the land of my oppression,
from favoring death to the desert,
or from living as what I'm not—
enslaved, orphaned, trapped.
For you, O Redeemer, have set me free,
called me child,

and secured a wide berth about me.
May I live brought out, beloved, and unleavened.

God who turns his eyes toward me,
may I turn mine toward you,
when a way can't be seen,
when the bitterness won't break,
when I've forgotten I've forgotten you.

May the righting of my memory, vision, and identity magnify
your unparalleled power,
and the story of the Redeemer, Transcendent, and Father
who sees and hears and saves.

Amen.

Chapter 2

THANKSGIVING

To Those Awaiting Harvest

He brought us into this place and gave us this land, a land flowing
with milk and honey. And behold, now I bring the first of the fruit of
the ground, which you, O LORD, have given me. And you shall set it
down before the LORD your God and worship before the Lord your God.

DEUTERONOMY 26:9-10

The air at harvest time felt different. Or was that anticipation? Months had passed since fall's planting season—months of waiting and praying for rain. Overwintering crops meant that for several months the ground lay dormant. It looked as though nothing would grow at all; you could barely tell anything had been planted.

Those empty fields held the hopes of an agrarian people dependent on the land for survival. Not only did the land provide their food; it was part of their national identity. The skies would not determine their fate, as neighboring nations believed, but their God—ruler over sky and earth and rain—who had given them the land and would cause rain to fall on it. He alone caused growth; abundance or plenty was out of their hands. So they waited for the first signs of new growth. As time went by, the fields became windblown seas of amber. They watched for the harvest to ripen for reaping.

Year after year, harvest after harvest, it would have been all too easy, without otherwise pausing, to forget about the Giver, to believe the harvest was all their doing. They won the land, they worked the land, they reaped its fruit with their own hands—so the story would become. As generations went by, the land and its abundance would have simply been "theirs" since they knew no other. But with each harvest, they paused to acknowledge the land's true owner. The land that fed them, clothed them, and energized them was God-given.

THANKFULNESS FADES

As we move from Passover to the spring festivals of the Feast of Firstfruits and Feast of Weeks, we travel from promise to fulfillment. Passover celebrated the momentous end to Israel's Egyptian captivity. It memorialized the strong hand and outstretched arm that led them through the sea. But once on the other side, 40 years would pass before they entered the land God promised them. While they were still in the wilderness, God told them how they were to celebrate once they left its trials behind.

When they did finally enter Canaan—the very day after they arrived— God's provision of manna ceased because he would now feed them from the land (Joshua 5:11-12). He had opened heaven to feed them miraculously in the wilderness where his hand was easier to see. Now he'd continue to feed them, but through the ordinary means of the soil beneath them, where his hand could be harder to see. God wanted Israel to remember he was still the one feeding them, so he decreed a feast of firstfruits, a sacred day recognizing his ongoing work sustaining his people.

The annual acknowledgment they were only subleasing the land doubled as a reminder of who God was—Israel's ultimate provider—and who they were as a result—a people who give thanks to God for all things. Further, these national celebrations "afforded opportunity for the

Israelites to renew their allegiance to God and to promote national unity."[1] Thanksgiving, identity, fulfillment, and unity all converged in this feast.

Once we've finally received a long-awaited gift from God, we strain to remember the wilderness or waiting season we left behind. Thankfulness quickly fades. God wanted Israel to know that he was behind where they were and what they now possessed. He tells them in Deuteronomy 6:10-12,

> When the LORD your God brings you into the land that he swore to your fathers, to Abraham, to Isaac, and to Jacob, to give you—with great and good cities that you did not build, and houses full of all good things that you did not fill, and cisterns that you did not dig, and vineyards and olive trees that you did not plant—and when you eat and are full, then take care lest you forget the LORD.

How easy it is to forget that a now-taken-for-granted treasure was a gift.

This festival, more than the others, has undergone significant changes in meaning since its inception. It was first tied to agriculture, then to the giving of the Torah, and now, for the church, to the giving of the Holy Spirit. Even with these changes, its through line remained thanksgiving to God for sustenance. In giving these feasts to his people, God institutes occasions for them to pause, remember, and rejoice in the realities of their national redemptive story. While the Passover said, "Look what I delivered you from," the Feast of Firstfruits says, "Remember, I gave this promised land to you." Where the people lived off the land, they celebrated it.

People of the Land Celebrate the Giving of the Land

Leviticus 23 lays out instructions for celebrating the Feast of Firstfruits. It was among the appointed feasts of the Lord instituted through

Moses: "Speak to the people of Israel and say to them, These are the appointed feasts of the LORD that you shall proclaim as holy convocations; they are my appointed feasts" (Leviticus 23:2). Twice in one sentence, God claims these festivals as his: they are "of the LORD" and "my appointed feasts." These festivals weren't meant to be celebrations of nationhood divorced from their founder. Rather, since God had instituted the festivals, he was their honoree.[2]

Not only did this festival require a sacrifice of the people's yield, but also a sacrifice of their time. Holy convocations were holidays where people rested from their work. "The setting apart of these holy days did not indicate that other days were not important, but they did serve as a reminder that all time belonged to God."[3] Their fields and their days were God's.

The Feast of Firstfruits' signature feature, being a harvest festival, involved presenting to the Lord the first of their barley harvest, planted in the fall around the first rain. It was a hardy crop—drought tolerant, able to grow in poor soil, and disease resistant—and was a staple grain of ancient Israel. They were essentially the dandelions of the cereal crops, being hard to kill. That made them a popular and relatively dependable crop, both for human and animal consumption. Next to wheat, barley had the longest sow-to-reap wait time of the agricultural calendar, as harvesters had to wait out the winter before seeing signs of growth.

THE SIGNIFICANCE OF FIRSTFRUITS

Firstfruits signified thankfulness. But there was also something important by virtue of their being first. The first of land and womb were ceremonially given back to God. Firstborn sons and animals, firstfruits of the ground—these firsts held a privileged position in the Hebrew Bible, as they were all set apart and made holy for the Lord. But especially with the firstfruits of the land, "The presentation of the first sheaf was representative of the entire crop, acknowledging that the yield came from the hand of God. God was to be honored with the firstfruits from the harvest to acknowledge that he graciously bestows blessings on the human race."[4] The Israelites were to bring a sheaf of barley to the priest, and he would wave the sheaf before the Lord "so that they could be accepted" (Leviticus 23:11). Besides the wave offering, several additional offerings were required: a burnt offering, grain offering, food offering, and drink offering. All the fruit of the land was God's; he had blessed them with it, and they were simply giving back to him what was his.

Giving of the firstfruits was also a sign of trust, as they had no way to know what the full crop would yield. It was also a sign of honor, as the first were considered the best (Numbers 18:12). Giving God his portion first meant they trusted that, of the remainder, they would have what they needed in both volume and quality, "something that from a human perspective was far from certain given the people's utter dependence on the right amount of rainfall and so forth to give the best crop."[5] Giving the first was a risk.

Finally, the giving of firstfruits was a sacrifice. The Israelites couldn't eat any bread or barley products until they'd first brought God their firstfruits (Leviticus 23:14). It was not that they set aside the sheaf for the festival and then began to use the rest of the yield. They couldn't partake of any of it until the Lord had his first and the festival was over. What they offered back to God was the priority.

Feast of Weeks

Fifty days from the Feast of Firstfruits was the Feast of Weeks, or *Shavuot*. It was, along with Passover, one of the three pilgrimage feasts. The instructions for the Feast of Weeks say, "You shall count seven full weeks from the day after the Sabbath, from the day that you brought the sheaf of the wave offering. You shall count fifty days to the day after the seventh Sabbath" (Leviticus 23:15). At some point during the Feast of Unleavened Bread there was a Sabbath. The day after that Sabbath was the Feast of Firstfruits, the day when the sickle was first put to the grain and the people brought a sheaf for the wave offering. The Feast of Weeks was seven weeks after the wave offering, forty-nine days after the Feast of Firstfruits or fifty days from Unleavened Bread's Sabbath. This is where the festival got the name it is perhaps better known by, Pentecost, which is Greek for "fiftieth."

The Feast of Weeks celebrated the close of the wheat harvest. Although wheat was planted at the same time as barley, it ripened later, between May and June. Like the Feast of Firstfruits, it was a time to celebrate God's providence and provision. It was also meant to be celebrated only after they came into the land God promised. As opposed to commemorating a single event, like the Passover, it was an annual reminder that God causes all things to grow. It celebrated a process begun, sustained, and completed by God himself. While the Feast of the Firstfruits celebrated the beginning of the harvest, the Feast of Weeks signified its conclusion. God was sovereign over everything in between.

UNGLEANED EDGES

At the end of the instructions for the Feast of Weeks, God makes a special request on behalf of those who are without land or harvest of their own: "When you reap the harvest of your land, you shall not reap your field right up to its edge, nor shall you gather the gleanings after your harvest. You shall leave them for the poor and for the sojourner" (Leviticus 23:22).[6] Even in their feasting and celebrating, Israel should not forget those who were poor. Not only that, but just as the firstfruits were earmarked for God, the gleanings, or leftovers, were earmarked for the poor. Both were acts of thanksgiving. Both acknowledged that everything they had came from God. Both were sacrifices—"from a purely economic viewpoint," notes Jerram Barrs, "the command not to go through the fields a second time was very costly." And both honored their provider. God outlawed being ungenerous in forbidding the Israelites from going back over their fields again to catch what they missed. Barrs writes, "They were to make sure that the poor had plenty to eat at the time of harvest. There was no way to obey this demand without including the needy in one's family celebration of the festivals. These laws are beautiful in their requirement of generosity to those in need."[7]

If it is considered stealing from God to not give to him as he commands (Malachi 3:8), then we also steal from him when we pocket his allotment for those in need. An honest recognition that everything comes from God means you're simply funneling his resources where he desires. For the people of God, sharing with the poor is not about giving *your* resources to those in need. Tying the gleaning rule to the celebration of God's provision for his people makes clear that sharing with the poor is about giving *God's* resources to those in need. Festivities flowed from the recognition that what we have isn't ours. Margin was to share, not to indulge.

Even though most of us are probably not farmers, these festivals still speak to us. They speak to our need to acknowledge that everything we have comes from God—and in this day and age, the more frequent that reminder, the better. God wanted his people to be a grateful people. For us, each day brings its own harvest of time and resources that we go about allocating based usually by default on our belief that they are ours. Without even thinking, "my" gets attached to our time, our gifts, and our finances. If you're at all like me, more often than I'd like, by the time I've gotten to God—if I've gotten to him at all—I'm down to scraps. Together these festivals challenge us to be obedient to giving God the firstfruits of what he's given us and to giving our neighbor the surplus. Not spending to the last dime. This festival also encourages us to live and give out of the reality that God is in control of our harvest.

Israel did not remain an agrarian society forever, nor did the people always stay in their land. As their relationship with the land changed, so, too, did their relationship to these festivals. They adapted. And, as we saw with the original Feast of Weeks, what people lived off of, they celebrated. Something else would soon overtake the land in importance.

PEOPLE OF THE LAW CELEBRATE
THE GIVING OF THE LAW

Eventually, the Feast of Weeks came to be associated with the giving of the Law at Mount Sinai described in Exodus 19 and 20. This shift began with the expulsion of God's people from their land during the exile. Since the festival was tied to a land they no longer occupied, people began to look for other connections to those holy days in their calendar.

The giving of the Law at Mount Sinai was believed to have taken place around that same time of year as the Feast of Weeks, in the third month, and Jewish writings linked the two together, giving the festival a "contemporary motif."[8] That significant moment in Israel's history came to be associated with the Feast of Weeks, and the connection to agriculture became secondary.

Even with the new focus on the Law, the festival remains a day of thanks, but for "the gift of his perfect Law, which showed Israel the way to live a wise life that would be pleasing to God."[9] Being people of the Law was an honor and God had given them the Law for their flourishing and freedom. Dairy foods are traditionally eaten on this holiday because the Torah is likened to the milk and honey of the land. Celebrated this way, the Feast of Weeks was still a sacred day recognizing God's sacred and ongoing work sustaining his people. As with the land, not only did the Law nourish them, it was also part of their national identity.

For Jews today, the anniversary of receiving the Law is still the principal meaning behind this festival. The covenantal nature of the Law added another layer of meaning to Shavuot. Jewish people consider it a symbolic wedding day, where God married his people through the covenant made with them on Mount Sinai.

As Christians, we too can celebrate the giving of the Law. I often return to the words of the psalmist in Psalm 19:7, "The law of the Lord is perfect, reviving the soul" and James' description of God's Word as "the perfect law that gives freedom" (James 1:25 NIV). These remind me I find life and freedom in its pages. I, too, am nourished by the Law and locate my story within its pages. But the anniversary of its giving is not this festival's final form, and the Christian's journey to learning from these feasts doesn't stop here. As was true with the land and with the Law would be true of the Spirit: what the people live off of, they celebrate.

PEOPLE OF THE SPIRIT CELEBRATE THE GIVING OF THE SPIRIT

By the time those early Jewish believers gathered together on that fateful Pentecost described in Acts 2, the festival was already firmly established as the anniversary of Law. The giving of the Spirit marked two momentous occasions in the life of the church: the fulfillment of Joel's prophecy about speaking in tongues (Joel 2:28-32), but also about the promised indwelling nature of God's Spirit that comes with the new covenant. In Jeremiah, Ezekiel, and even as far back as Deuteronomy, God speaks of a new covenant he will make with his people.[10] That is a covenant Christians believe Christ ultimately fulfilled. When Jesus shares his final meal with his disciples, he says the cup is the new covenant in his blood. One feature of this new covenant is that the Law would no longer be written on tablets, but on the heart, and that God would put his Spirit within his people.

The apostles were on alert for some supernatural activity of God's Holy Spirit because Christ's last words to them before his ascension were that a new kind of baptism for them was on the way (Acts 1:4-5). Gathered on the day of Pentecost, days after that promise, the apostles and other followers of Jesus were interrupted—a loud sound like rushing wind just before tongues of fire rested on them and the Spirit filled them. The imagery such as wind and fire echoed Old Testament scenes in which God appeared to his people.[11] Wind was commonly linked to the work of the Spirit in the Old Testament as far back as Genesis 1:2. As the Spirit descended, the apostles began to speak other languages they did not know from around the region.

This occasion was the official launch of the global, Spirit-empowered church with members "from every nation, from all tribes and peoples and languages" (Revelation 7:9). Earlier Jesus gave his disciples the Great Commission, but now he gave them the power to carry it out. While the disciples were inside speaking foreign tongues, the multitude outside were bewildered, each hearing Galileans praise God in their own native languages. The regions represented on the list of passersby include locations of strategic importance to fulfilling the reach of the gospel to the ends of the earth. In his commentary on Acts, I. Howard Marshall writes that "the list is clearly meant to be an indication that people from all over the known world were present, and perhaps that they would return to their own countries as witnesses to what was happening."[12] From its inception, the church was multiethnic.

FIRSTFRUITS REVISITED

In 1 Corinthians 15:20, Paul describes Jesus as the "firstfruits of those who have fallen asleep." Christ was the first raised of the righteous. He was the waved sheaf pointing to a later, greater harvest of believers who would eventually be raised as well.

The Holy Spirit is also described as a firstfruit in Romans 8:23: "Not only the creation, but we ourselves, who have the firstfruits of the Spirit, groan inwardly as we wait eagerly for adoption as sons, the redemption of our bodies." As a firstfruit, the Spirit precedes an even fuller harvest in the future, where we are adopted as God's children. Elsewhere, Paul speaks of the Spirit as being a "down payment" or "deposit" guaranteeing a greater inheritance to come (2 Corinthians 1:22; 5:5; Ephesians 1:13-14). This is the language of "there's more."

The Holy Spirit seems to be the least well-known member of the Trinity. We say we live by him, but don't recognize all that encompasses. The Holy Spirit is our comforter. He helps us in our weakness and intercedes for us. He is the spout through which God's love has been poured into our hearts. He bears witness to us and to the world of who God is.

He surpasses the Law in grandeur and glory and by him the Law is now written on our hearts. With the indwelling Spirit, love for God and choosing obedience and life are possible. He guides us into all truth, empowers, and liberates us. He convicts and transforms, enlightens and makes wise. Because of the Spirit, we can know the mind of Christ.

The Holy Spirit is the beginning of our spiritual blessedness, not the end. He is the guarantee of things to come. He begins us and perfects us. He feeds and sustains us. He's the mark of a gifted sonship. He sets us apart as his people and gives life to our decaying bodies. He fills us with anticipation and hope and seals us for the day of redemption.

Through the Spirit, we access the Father and are united to other believers. He equips us each in distinct ways for the uplifting of the church and was given, in part, that we may better care for our neighbor in need. The Spirit bears within us the exotic fruit of love, joy, peace, patience, kindness, goodness, faithfulness, gentleness, and self-control—revolutionizing our love for our neighbor.

Landed, Lawed, Spirited

This feast of Pentecost took on a new meaning for Christians, but it remains a sacred day recognizing God's sacred and ongoing work sustaining his people. Where people live by the Spirit, they celebrate the Spirit. God remains the source of all we have and for that, we give him thanks. God's Word is dear to us as the people of God and for that we, too, give thanks. But what most sets us apart now as his treasured possession is not our land, nor our Law, but God's Spirit within us. This is our national pride as citizens of his kingdom. With the giving of the

Spirit, the celebration isn't disrupted but further enriched. We offer our firstfruits to the Lord and leave gleanings for those in need as a celebration of the one whose resources we steward. We celebrate the revelation of God's Word and its living, active power to move within our hearts and increase our knowledge of him.

God's Spirit is our crowning joy in this life, the long-awaited gift, our promised prosperity, our anticipated peace. Given the Spirit, we give thanks to God. Not annually, appearing with offerings before the priest, but every day, as Clement of Alexandria wrote: "The whole of life is a continual festival, insofar as it is entirely consecrated to God in an act of thanksgiving."[13] And with the giving of the Spirit, we travel from promise fulfilled back to promise made again, as it guarantees things greater to come. Greater joy, greater comfort, greater freedom, greater peace, and greater love for God and neighbor.

MORE ON THE WAY

One afternoon, I was considering getting takeout for dinner. I'd ordered takeout a lot and was trying to be mindful of my budget. Suddenly, I remembered my grandpa had called the other day to tell me he'd put a check for me in the mail. I perked up, nodding and grinning to myself, thinking, "His money's on the way." It ended up being a Korean fried chicken kind of night.

You just live different when you know there's more on the way. That's what the Holy Spirit says to our hearts, what he says to our time, what he says to our resources, what he says to all we possess: "There's more on the way." Since what we have in the Holy Spirit is far surer and more certain than what the ancient Israelites had in their fields, our anticipation of a bountiful harvest should far exceed theirs. So we overwinter here on earth, where, for long stretches, growth seems elusive and conditions frigid, as we look forward to that great future day of reaping.

LITURGY FOR PROVISION

The eyes of all look to you, and you give
them their food in due season.

PSALM 145:15

Lord of seed, growth, and harvest,
thank you for the land that sustains me
and is a sign of your yet unfolding promise.
All eyes look to you in season for their food.
You open your hand and you satisfy.
May I never grow complacent with your gifts
or lapse into feeling self-made.
May I not cut my neighbor off from the corner of my field
or commit any injustice with your land and profane it.
Even when these bequeathed fields withhold their yield
and dry earth demands deepened trust,
keep me from unbelief and fill me from your bottomless
stores.

Lord of Law who liberates,
thank you for sustaining me through your Word
and for using your Law as a guardian to lead me to Christ.
My soul searches your Word for food,
You open my mind and you supply.
Your Word is penetrating and active,
grant me a heart of good soil to absorb it.

May it bud and sprout where you plant it
and flower in the crevices of my soul.
May I do no injustice with your Word,
withholding it from those in need.

Lord of indwelling Spirit,
thank you for living through us.
You renew us, regenerate us, and have sealed us.
We look to you to learn God's gratuity,
and you translate it in time to our hearts.
You ready us for our wedding day,
you give freedom and comfort today.
May we not withhold your fruit from our neighbors
or through neglect stunt its growth.
May your Spirit make us as one body,
bidding all harmful divisions cease.

God of our survival,
of seed, growth, and harvest,
of liberating Law and indwelling Spirit,
thank you for this gift of gifting those in need,
and may our clearest expression of thanksgiving
be lives lived in humble dependence on you.

Chapter 3

FALL FEASTS OF ATONEMENT AND JOY

To the Unclean

It shall be a statute to you forever that in the seventh month, on the tenth day of the month, you shall afflict yourselves and shall do no work, either the native or the stranger who sojourns among you. For on this day shall atonement be made for you to cleanse you. You shall be clean before the LORD from all your sins. It is a Sabbath of solemn rest to you, and you shall afflict yourselves; it is a statute forever.

LEVITICUS 16:29-31

On the eve of Yom Kippur, the high priest stayed up through the night to ensure he did not become unclean in his sleep. All Israel was relying on him, as he was the only one who could perform the rites of the feast the next day. The Feast of Trumpets nine days earlier had initiated a time of preparation for the holiest day of the year, and now that day was upon them.

In the morning, the high priest dressed in his priestly robes. By rote, he performed the daily morning rites: burnt offering, grain offering, drink offering. The lamps in the tabernacle were checked. Fresh incense was burned on the altar fire. To the priests, every day was a day for slaughter, but this day was different, and the gravity of its duties weighed heavily upon him.

The high priest then bathed before changing into his special Yom Kippur linens—humble compared to his usual priestly regalia.[1] He assembled the sacrifices needed for the day and cast lots to see which of the two goats set apart for the day would become a sacrifice to God at the tabernacle and which would be banished to the wilderness. With the preparatory work behind him, he carefully reviewed, for the hundredth time, the protocol for what was about to take place.

He first presented a bull as a sin offering for himself and his household. He must first be clean. At the tabernacle's entrance, he placed a hand on the head of the bull and slaughtered it, being careful not to break any of its bones or get any of its blood on his garments. He set some blood aside in a small bowl to take with him behind the veil.

With a smoking censer in one hand and two handfuls of sweet incense in the other, he approached the veil. He was alone; no other priests were permitted to accompany him this day. Behind the veil, one misstep could mean death. He pulled the veil back and paused to let his eyes adjust to the dark. The holy of holies. He used the censer and incense to create a cloud protecting him from the intense glory and holiness of the mercy seat—the lid of pure gold with two cherubim carved into its sides that covered the ark of the covenant. God's presence hovered above it. Penitent, the high priest dipped his fingers in the blood and sprinkled it before the mercy seat seven times.

The process repeated with the sin offering for the people, except this time with a goat. This sacrifice purged the Holy Place of the uncleanness of the people. The high priest sprinkled the goat's blood before the altar of burnt offering. Then, after he and his household, the people, the Holy Place, the altar, and the tabernacle were all atoned for, the second goat was led by a handler into the wilderness. But first, the high priest confessed the sins of the people over it and transferred them to his head.

The next day, Israel broke their fast and had only a few days to construct a shelter, *sukkah*, for Sukkot. The structure was intentionally bare: three undecorated walls and a covering made of unaffixed branches, with space left in between to let in sunlight and rain. Family members would search for materials. The walls could be made of anything but needed to be sturdy enough to withstand fall winds. Children would help gather myrtle branches for the roof. For seven days, the family would eat and pray together in that structure, and at night they slept looking up at the sky through the sparse branch roofing. The sojourner, the fatherless, and the widow were also to be included in the feast. Sukkot, the last of the three fall festivals, commemorated Israel's wandering in the desert and the time of their humbling.

FALL FEASTS

The Feast of Trumpets, Yom Kippur, and Sukkot coincided with the end of fall harvest season, giving them both agricultural and theological significance like the spring feasts. The Feast of Trumpets and Yom Kippur are considered the High Holy Days of the Jewish religious calendar. Rather than centering on wheat or barley, the fall harvest was grapes, figs, and olives. *Tishri,* the seventh month of the Israelite calendar, corresponds to September or October in the Gregorian calendar. The Feast of Trumpets is better known as Rosh Hashanah, the Jewish New Year. Yom Kippur is also known as the Day of Atonement. And Sukkot is also called the Feast of Tabernacles or Booths.

These fall feasts are rich with significance. Each one points to the redeeming work of the Messiah. The Feast of Trumpets called for judgment and self-examination in advance of the holiest of days. Yom Kippur encompassed the forgiveness and transfer of our sins to a substitute, enabling God to continue dwelling among his people. It was a feast for purification and the most solemn day of the year, the Sabbath of sabbaths. And Sukkot was a kind of reenactment of Israel's wandering years, where God provided for their every need, just as Christ does ours.

FEAST OF TRUMPETS

Sound is powerful. Film composers labor over capturing and creating a movie's story through sound. The Feast of Trumpets was part of the soundtrack of the religious life of Israel. Other sounds might be the bleating of animal sacrifices; songs and liturgies for set days; the timbrel, pipe, and harp. Sound, like food, can transport you back to significant moments and seasons of life. For Israel, the ram's horn did just that.

As we've seen, feasts can look backward or forward. With the appointed feasts of Israel, they often do both. One purpose of blowing a horn traditionally used for war was to remind Israel of God's past triumphs. Richard Booker writes, "To the Hebrews, the sound of the trumpet represented both the voice of God and the might of God in warfare."[2] As time went on, the number and importance of those victories would grow, as would the need to memorialize them.

Looking forward, the sacred day of judgment and atonement was fast approaching. The horn served as an alert, like the ding of a reminder set in your calendar to leave on time or to help you prepare. Securing sacrifices, undertaking travel, and reconciling with one's neighbor are all actions this horn blast triggered. Preparations had to be made.

YOM KIPPUR

Yom Kippur was meant to facilitate God's continued presence among his people. The accumulated sin of God's people risked making the tabernacle unfit for his presence. The day's rites, if followed down to the jot and tittle, would bring the high priest safely into the closest proximity to God on earth possible, into the Holy of Holies. They would give the sanctuary the deep cleanse it required.

But the day was not solely about the high priest and his actions. It was about the disposition of the people. In the days leading up to Yom Kippur from the Feast of Trumpets, had they sought the forgiveness of those they'd offended? Had they righted wrong ways of neighboring? Did they feel remorse over their sin? Would they bring into the momentous day only their bodies but not their hearts?

Atonement was not a new concept to Israel when Yom Kippur was instituted in Leviticus 16. The sacrificial system God had given them already included the sin offering. Leviticus 4:1–5:13 details what was required for the sin offering and includes the refrain about the priest making atonement for the people. What stood out about Yom Kippur, however, was how it expanded what Israel knew about atonement, sin offerings, and even holiness while inherently hinting at the system's limits.

The instructions for the Day of Atonement in Leviticus 16 follow several chapters listing purity and cleanliness laws (Leviticus 11–15). Certain animals and objects couldn't be touched. Contact with specific kinds of diseases was prohibited. There were rules for purification after childbirth, housecleaning, and bodily discharge. As rule piled upon rule, it was a wonder anyone could meet the Law's demands at all. Cleanliness was impossible.

On this day when God essentially deep cleaned his house and his people, no one but the high priest could assist. As a Sabbath of sabbaths, the strict contrast between God's role and the Israelites' in atonement could not have been more stark. God does all the work.

Yom Kippur pointed to the work of Christ. It granted the closest access to God, forgave the widest range of sin, and provided a vivid picture of substitution. It also emphasized the absolute purity and gravity of the holiness of God. The minute detail in the day's ritual and the exclusivity of access reinforced this idea. But simultaneously, its annual nature hinted it was of limited effect. It had a purpose for its time and did what only it could do at that time. Yom Kippur raised issues Christ alone solved.

For the ancient Israelites, the highest level of access to God was available to only one person on only one day each year. What's more, the tabernacle was earthly, made of human hands, a shadow of the heavenly one after which it was patterned. As sinful, the priest had first to make sacrifices for himself. Only then could he enter the presence of God and only by means of the blood of bulls or goats. Most importantly, the gifts and sacrifices he offered could not perfect the conscience (Hebrews 9:9), itself a heavenly counterpart to the flesh (Hebrews 9:23). Being ceremonially clean was external, while a cleansed conscience went straight to the core. Rather than penetrating deep, according to the author of Hebrews, Yom Kippur offerings were concerned with matters of clean and unclean food and drink and various ceremonial washings (Hebrews 9:10). The conscience was impenetrable by even that most sacred and encompassing of old covenant sacrifices.

But in Christ, a new way opened for access to God that improved upon all the old system's weaknesses (Hebrews 10:20). In his perfection, Christ entered the true holy of holies once, and once only, by none other than his own blood to purify us once and for all. How potent the blood that it alone now enables us to truly and routinely draw near to God's throne, to have an audience with the King of kings. Not only can we come, but we can come as we are. And he who dwells in unapproachable light does not strike us down or turn us away but listens to our every petition. New Testament scholar George Caird explains, "The sacrifices of the old covenant were a perpetual reminder of sin and of man's need of atonement, but what men needed was the effective removal of sin, so that it could no longer barricade the way into the inner presence of God."[3] In the new system under Christ, our access level has changed and we can now go directly to God to find grace and mercy in our time of need (Hebrews 4:16). Atonement ultimately points to the breadth and efficacy of Christ's blood. One drop could cleanse for all time for all people for all sin what the blood of a million unblemished bulls could not do for one person once.

Through Yom Kippur, we gain a deeper appreciation for the holiness of God. The elaborate sacrificial system, of which Yom Kippur was the crown, was required because God is holy and we are not. His holiness cannot abide with our unholiness. In the old covenant, we could never have shared in or approached his holiness. At best, we could try in our own strength to emulate it. But our very fallen nature polluted the tabernacle. This is why the tabernacle itself, made by human hands, had to be atoned for.

SUKKOT

Sukkot, as mentioned, commemorated the time of Israel's wandering in the desert. The people of Israel constructed tiny booths, or *sukkah*, outside to live in for a week as a temporary shelter.

Wandering humbles us. Wandering makes us dependent on God and divorces us from the comforts of the world. The wilderness is the optimal location to prove God's unseen hand. What other location lays our hearts so bare? Where else can so distinctly set hearts on the promised glory to come?

If the Passover was about God delivering Israel out of Egypt, Sukkot was about what happened on the far side of the Red Sea. Israel's journey out of captivity and into the land God promised them is central in the history of redemption. It was, at that time and for generations afterward, the pièce de résistance of God's mighty works. He would cite this as part of his royal epithet: the God who brought his people out of the land of Egypt (Exodus 20:2). From the perspective of his people, "Sukkot commemorates the maturation of the Israelites, achieved not in crossing the Red Sea but in walking the long way to freedom."[4] Their delivery was both instantaneous yet progressively unfolding. They were no longer slaves in Egypt, but not yet residents of Canaan. Sukkot represents that time in between, Israel's journey to freedom through dependence on God.

Like the Feast of Weeks, it contained a provision for the most vulnerable portions of their community on the margins. Servants were to join families in celebrations, but so too were the sojourner, the fatherless, and the widow within their towns (Deuteronomy 16:14). Generosity was built into the feast, yet another example that God cares for those at the margins and wants his people to keep them in their view. All three of the pilgrimage feasts include provisions for the less fortunate and marginalized. For those to suffer neglect while the well-off rejoice would be incongruous. This day was about the dependence of a vulnerable people on God's grace. How could they be recipients of such grace without being channels of it too? How could they honor and dishonor God at the same time?

Sukkot is also known as *zman simchateinu,* the "season of our rejoicing." Contrary to Yom Kippur, a feast of deep contrition, this was a feast of unbridled joy. It was a study in contrasts. Repentance and self-reflection were called for, but on their heels, joy of a robustness not commanded elsewhere was to follow. The instructions for the feast given in Deuteronomy says, "You shall rejoice in your feast," and for seven days they shall be "altogether joyful" (Deuteronomy 16:13, 15). Joy was an imperative. What joy, though, did wandering hold?

First, in God's provision and second, in the glory of the promise. God provided for the Israelites in the desert. God did not abandon them, but led them by day and by night, giving them his "good Spirit to instruct them" (Nehemiah 9:20). God fed them the bread of angels for their hunger and did not withhold water for their thirst (Psalm 78:25). For 40 years he sustained them, "they lacked nothing, their clothes did not wear out nor did their feet become swollen" (Nehemiah 9:21) or their sandals fray (Deuteronomy 29:5).

I live in a walkable city and don't own a car. I walk almost everywhere. Try as I might, I cannot get a pair of halfway decent shoes to survive more than 10 or 11 months without the soles detaching from the sides. Here was a whole community of people who, for their entire lives, had just one pair of sandals. If that isn't faithfulness, I don't know what is.

It may seem counterintuitive to reenact hardship, but perhaps not if the grace you received to survive more than made up for the grief. Frederick Buechner writes,

> To remember my life is to remember countless times when I might have given up, gone under, when humanly speaking I might have gotten lost beyond the power of any to find me. But I didn't. I have not given up. And each of you, with all the memories you have and the tales you could tell, you also have not given up. You also are survivors and are here. And what does that tell us, our surviving? It tells us that weak as we are, a strength beyond our strength has pulled us through at least this far, at least to this day.[5]

Sukkot is an embodied communal remembering of our God-wrought survival.

Dwelling temporarily in intentionally spare tents symbolizes that their wandering was but for a time and that although they felt vulnerable, they were actually protected. "Jews learned that the *Shechinah* (Divine Presence) is with them in areas of wandering as well as during the triumphant return to the Holy Land."[6] It reminds us our perception of reality does not always align with truth, that hardship has an end, and that there's more than the material.

> In all this you greatly rejoice, though now for *a little while* you may have had to suffer grief in all kinds of trials. These have come so that the proven genuineness of your faith—of greater worth than gold, which perishes even though refined by fire—may result in praise, glory, and honor when Jesus Christ is revealed. Though you have not seen him, you love him; and even though you do not see him now, you believe in him and are filled with an inexpressible and glorious joy, for you are receiving the end result of your faith, the salvation of your souls (1 Peter 1:6-9).

We can trust God in the wilderness.

I wandered through my own wilderness for years, struggling to see God's hand, struggling to know and feel his presence, questioning his path even though I had no better. Joy hides in the ability to see the unseen, to choose to trust when situations seem impossible. For Jews at Sukkot, "By deliberately giving up solid construction, Jews admit their vulnerability and testify that the ultimate trust is in the divine shelter."[7] Like the Israelites, I lobbed distrustful accusations against him: "You have brought me into this desert to starve me to death" (Exodus 16:3), and "Why did you bring me up out of Egypt to make me die of thirst?" (Exodus 17:3). I wandered in and out of my own Massah and Meribah, lands of complaining and strife, wondering, "Is the Lord with me or not?" (Exodus 17:7).

In the wilderness, the Israelites constantly questioned whether God was with them or not, which implies that their questions about water and food and location to camp were ultimately ones of presence. They did not doubt God's cosmic sovereignty as much as his nearness and concern for them. As Israel dwelt in temporary *sukkah* to celebrate Sukkot, we too, in our earthly tents, groan and long for our heavenly dwelling and seek shelter in the Spirit, our deposit guaranteeing Christ's return (2 Corinthians 5:4-5). Has joy greater impetus than this?

SUKKOT TODAY

Sukkot challenges us to reframe our wilderness. There will be times that God follows up a great victory with a small, confusing, or unexpected disappointment. Or where obedience sends us head-first into failure. Or where what we fear most comes true. Is it not a comfort in our wilderness that we can approach his throne of grace with confidence to find grace and mercy in our time of need? Does not the intimacy of God make less bleak the inhospitable, barren wilderness?

Even now, more broadly, we live in the in-between "already/not yet" space. This threadbare world we now inhabit is our *sukkah*. And this time—the time between our Egypt and our promised land—is our *zman simchateinu,* the season of our rejoicing. We've been delivered from the kingdom of darkness to the kingdom of light. But though we are citizens there, here we reside, looking forward to a "one day" home we have only felt within us.

The Sukkot way was to make the *sukkah* a bit bare. They could not be built under anything else, such as an awning or tree, that might provide additional protection from the elements. They were not to make them so sturdy that no trust in God would be needed. Their construction said, "Let this tent be a tent, and God be your god."

So often we try to force onto the temporary a stability only possible through the eternal. We look to relationships, careers, wealth, image, or power to define and fulfill us. We give them the last word on our worth, tying both our value and God's faithfulness to how much of each we have. But *sukkah* staked in these transient matters produce desperation, while *sukkah* pitched in God produce rest. Trying to make indestructible castles of *sukkah* will catch up with us in the end. All such structures are inherently unsound. But if we let our *sukkah* stand as is, it drives us, instead, to trust.

As it is, we often God-proof our lives. That's not to say we reject God, but we avoid being the one on the boat with our foot hovering above the water. We live to minimize risk; there's little we're trusting God for. And while we don't want to create emergencies, there are ways we can build room for trust in our lives. We can be generous, especially with our money, but also with our time and other prized resources. Hospitality was built into the practice of Sukkot, of bringing more into your booth than you needed so you could share what you had with others.

God with Us

As Christians, seeing these special days in light of Christ heightens their meaning. They enrich our appreciation of Christ's blood. They remind us of the wonder of hosting the Holy Spirit—God himself—within us and receiving him among us and of how profound it is we have an audience with him.

Both feasts are about God's presence: the maintaining of his presence through cleansing sacrifices and his sustaining presence while we wander the wilderness. We see God is holy and active in our lives, atoning, guiding, reminding. These feasts speak to the centrality, efficacy, and sufficiency of God's presence.

They also speak to the attitude of our hearts in light of that presence which brings deep contrition, grief over sin, and solemnity—and, in turn, consummate joy, bliss at our freedom, and trust. God set the tone for each of these feasts with the blast of a horn, a fast, and a call for rejoicing. He gives us seasons to prepare, reflect, and rejoice.

Sukkot is the culmination of religious festivals God gave his people. It ends with a celebration of the long road of dependence to the promised land.

LITURGY FOR GOD'S PRESENCE

ATONEMENT

God Most High,
I have transgressed your laws:
what my eyes have seen,
my hands have touched,
my ears have heard,
my mind has thought,
my heart has desired.
I have tried, but still fall short.
On my own, I'm unworthy
to approach your throne.
Instead, I cry, "Unclean! Unclean! Unclean!"

Yet in your mercy, you made a way
to open your most holy throne to me
by sending your Son in my likeness
to fulfill your righteous standard
and offer himself, a blood sacrifice
from an indestructible life.
You call back, "Be clean, be clean, be clean."

So made worthy I draw near
and marvel at your throne,
seeking grace and mercy
in my time of need.
By your Spirit deep clean my heart, O God,
and make your home within me.

Sukkot[8]

Sovereign Guide of our wilderness,
You divided the sea and let us pass,
by your rescue you've given us life.
Led with cloud by day and fire by night,
by your guidance you've given us life.
Turning rocks into rivers and giving us drink,
quenching our thirst you've given us life.
Spreading a table in the desert and brought us to safety,
by protecting us you've given us life.
When we're prone to doubt and you're gentle with us,
by your patience you've given us life.

Chapter 4

A Victory Celebration

To the ~~Defeated~~

> *You prepare a table before me in the presence of my*
> *enemies, you anoint my head with oil, my cup overflows.*
>
> PSALM 23:5

The feasts of the Bible do not end with Israel's special holy days. Poets and sages take up the theme of feasting as well, but to describe their everyday experience of God. Within the span of the six well-beloved verses of Psalm 23, we shadow a sheep led by tranquil waters, sustained through a perilous valley, and shielded from predators. Third-person "he" changes to more intimate "you" in the valley, as we shift from hearing public testimony to private praise. We celebrate victory with the psalmist at a banquet table and marvel at the host's provision. We watch as goodness and mercy, which cannot be outrun or escaped, give him chase. At long last, we reach the very house of the Lord, the perfection of every proximate place of peace and safety. In these few verses, we are swung between danger and delight, each moment accompanied by the Lord.

Psalm 23's evocative richness and sure-footed claims have made it the most beloved of the psalter. In it, the tired find comfort and the besieged, safety. It contains not a single supplication but boast upon boast in the Lord. Psalms of confidence emerge from a soul that's chosen to tread the narrow path to trust. "Despite circumstances" goes without saying. The Twenty-Third Psalm exemplifies unflinching confidence amidst hardship and the firmest conviction that all will be well.

Each metaphor—that of shepherd and sheep, host and guest—bears partial burden of conveying the psalm's overall message of provision and protection through God's tender presence in the face of danger. "I shall not want," the earliest of the psalmist's boasts, is emphatic in the Hebrew. Whether in pasturelands, valleys, or battlegrounds, this boast holds true. At the heart of the psalm, we find the reason: "for you are with me." As Futato puts it, "The rest of the psalm fills in the details of this magnificent portrait of the beneficent presence of a personal God."[1]

A Shepherd with His Sheep

The psalmist couldn't be more convinced of and cheered by his shepherd's nearness. Presence was blessing enough, but he also knew that with it came refreshment and security. Facing scarcity, he could rely on his shepherd to be right there, leading the way to abundance. Lying rather than just feeding in green pastures implies abundance: "They have eaten, are satisfied, and have no need to move on to look for further grass: this pasture will provide the next meal, too."[2] The waters of repose likewise suggest sufficiency: "The sheep may drink and lie down by the pool, again knowing they can get up and have another drink."[3] Through the green pastures and restful waters, the psalmist's life returns to him, and he can continue along right paths.

Facing danger, the psalmist was confident his shepherd was alert to threats and could lead him to safety. Lying down also implied a lowered guard and increased sense of security, as Scripture often pairs this posture with safety and the absence of fear (Leviticus 26:6; Job 11:19; Psalm 4:8; Isaiah 17:2; Ezekiel 34:14-15; Hosea 2:18; Zephaniah 3:13). As for the valley, many a sheep with an inferior shepherd fainted at the specter of death; but his shepherd's rod calmed, his staff cleared the way. Buechner notes the shift to second person in verse four, "Here at the very center of the psalm comes the very center of the psalmist's faith. Suddenly he stops speaking about God as 'he,'...and he speaks to him as 'thou.' 'I will fear no evil,' he says, 'for thou art with me.' That is the center of faith. Thou. That is where faith comes from."[4]

A Host with His Guest

But the wonders of his Lord were only half told. Beyond food and drink, beyond vigor, beyond even safe passage through darkness, his Lord could throw a banquet on a battlefield. While pastures and valleys likely come quickest to most people's minds when they think of this psalm, the psalmist's confidence doesn't end at the mouth of the valley. As the psalmist continues to draw from images he knows best, we get a scene of hostility juxtaposed with the "unfettered enjoyment of the presence of God."[5] The ambient calm, contentment, and fearlessness of the flock spill over onto the image of a feast fit for a king.

The psalm's intensity does not ebb in its second half, but rather swells. Spurgeon suggests that the imagery of the feast surpasses even that of the pastureland in expressing restfulness: "It is the very acme of security and repose that is here described. I know of no expression, not even that of lying down in green pastures, that is more full of restfulness than this: 'Thou preparest a table before me in the presence of mine enemies.'"[6] And although the two metaphors share themes of abundance and protection, the table moves us beyond the survival of the valley. "It is one thing to survive a threat, as in verse four; quite another to turn it into triumph,"[7] Kidner writes. The table intensifies the first half of the psalm's claims.

The table is a brazen victory declaration, a defiant parade of unmatched resources conspicuously displayed before his enemies, but before the psalmist under assault it is a balm. Kidner continues, "Every detail here is in that key, from the wealth at table to the festive oil and brimming cup. The picture may be one of calm assurance under pressure, an Old Testament equivalent of Romans 8:31-39 or 2 Corinthians 12:9f; A witness to infinite resources in the worst of situations."[8] This is a table not set just for survival, but for pleasure. Wine gladdens the heart, and fragrant oil poured on the head refreshed one's guest.

The shared obligation of shepherd and host to look after those in their care binds the two metaphors thematically together. In the Ancient Near East, it was standard for hosts to take responsibility for their guest's protection and well-being. An invitation to a meal doubled as an offer of sanctuary. Just as shepherds protect their sheep, hosts would've been expected to provide protection and shelter for their guests—as the Genesis 19 account of Lot hosting two angels disguised as men demonstrates. When the townspeople come to Lot's house intent on harming his guests, he says to them, "Only do nothing to these men, for they have come under the shelter of my roof" (Genesis 19:8).

ROYALTY

This was no common hospitality. An air of royalty pervades this psalm. In the Old Testament, kings were often referred to as shepherds (1 Chronicles 17:6; Zechariah 10:3; 2 Samuel 7:7; Ezekiel 37:24). Within the broader Ancient Near Eastern context, Beth LaNeel Tanner notes a connection with the Babylonian king of the gods. "The image of the shepherd providing peaceful waters for the flock," she writes, "is stock language with royal overtones, as the description of Marduk as the one 'who provides grazing and drinking places' demonstrates."[9] Most Old Testament references to a table refer to a king's table, and in many of these cases, a king graciously extends a seat at their table to non-royalty.

Royalty came with wealth. While the psalms, by nature, use highly figurative language, the table is both concrete and abstract. In average domestic use, people served food on a large piece of leather. Only wealthy homes had the wooden dining furniture we imagine when we hear the word *table*. *Table* was also a stand-in expression for "the bowls and goblets laden with rich food and exquisite elixirs"[10]—in other words, a feast. Most references to feasts in the Old Testament do not explicitly mention a table. Instead, they focus on specific foods or another element of the festivities. The table in Psalm 23 signifies ample supply and an uncommonly well-off host. At that table, as in the pasturelands and valleys, the psalmist does not want.

Loyalty

It's not just about *what* they have at the table but *who,* and the psalmist has God. At the Lord's table, our battles become his and his victories become ours. In Exodus 23:22, God promises, "I will be an enemy to your enemies and an adversary to your adversaries." The Lord our host is our ally. Those are the terms of the covenant. "I will bless those who bless you, and him who dishonors you I will curse, and in you all the families of the earth shall be blessed" (Genesis 12:3). At the table, alliances were formed and loyalties reaffirmed. He does not stand back from heaven and plot, but rather, Psalm 23:5 shows him setting a place at his table for us. He draws near to fill and to feed, and to flood the soul with his grace. To provide, as it were, "ultimate communion with God himself"[11] and ultimate protection from our adversaries, who can no longer do us harm.

The psalmist inverts the enemy theme as the Lord dispatches goodness and mercy to attend him instead. The same single-minded pursuit an enemy brings to their battle, goodness and mercy bring to their blessing. He needn't fear capture by enemy but can look forward to capture by grace.

Goodness and mercy do exactly what they've been divinely dispatched to do: carry the psalmist to the abode of his supreme host and true refuge. God is the terminus to the psalmist's every journey, and he is reached only by the psalmist's faith working in tandem with God's goodness and mercy.

DEFEAT AND VICTORY DEFINED

Several years ago, my job was on the line and some of my colleagues were actively working to see me get let go. I learned from a friend that one of them was boasting about it at parties. Every day I went into work unsure of who I could trust. As I prayed to God about the situation—for favor, for the frustrated plans of those who wished me ill, that I would keep my job—I kept being drawn back to Scripture about loving my enemies. I wanted to triumph over them, but the Lord said: "Do good to those who hate you, bless those who curse you, pray for those who mistreat you" (Luke 6:26-27 NIV). This was absolutely not what I wanted to hear, but it became my prayer and mission anyway.

Months later, I lost my job. It took 15 months to find a new one. But to the end, I loved my ill-intentioned colleagues well. To me, that was victory.

We often have a skewed sense of victory. Does an honest loss beat dishonest gain? Does taming the tongue beat getting the last word? Does being wise in the things of God beat possessing the wisdom of this world? Does following God, eyes wide open into hardship, beat taking detours that skirt discipline or discomfort? Is the fleeting taste of victory the world offers sweeter to us than the victory we have in Christ? And do we find more meat on the decomposing bones of worldly triumph than we do on the broken flesh of our Savior? Whose "Well done" are we even living for?

If we cannot recognize the difference between victory and defeat, if we don't know who or what the real enemy is, then the truly defeated will reject the table thinking they've won, while the truly victorious will believe that they've lost. Though the world may confuse the two, followers of Jesus, those who know the real Victor and the real enemy, should not. It's not that God is trying to get us to perform mental gymnastics to see victory differently. It's not a matter of seeing differently at all but seeing *correctly*. He's not redefining our understanding of victory, but resetting it to factory settings, disencumbering it from the falsehoods of the world.

THE CROSS AND THE TABLE

The cross is the clearest picture we have of triumph. It teaches us that winning often looks like losing. Like the table in the psalm, it too is a sign of loyalty, royalty, provision, and victory. It is our boast before our enemies and a mid-battle reminder that victory is secure even if not yet in hand. It's a celebration of what's ours because we're his. It's evidence of the goodness, faithfulness, friendship, and generous hospitality of God. The king, the planks of wood, the onlooking enemies, the true nourishment available—all these images of the table in the psalm point to the cross. Even the potential for reconciliation, as some scholars suggest this passage hints at, are displayed in the cross that at once, and quite beautifully, illustrates both victory and prevailing peace.

Neither the cross nor the table erases our troubles. But what overrides them is God's being with us and for us in its midst.

> We need to acknowledge to ourselves and others that being in Christ does not mean that the troubles, cares, pains, and dangers of this world are simply removed from us. We remain "in the presence" of our enemies. We need also, however, to ask and constantly remind

ourselves in what ways, day by day, God is setting a table
for us in the presence of our enemies.[12]

We feast in his presence, even as our enemies loiter in sight.

Our spot at the everyday victory feasts Christ spreads for us is what
is daily at stake on the wide path of disbelief before us. If we don't know
what victory is, we'll miss God's invitation to celebrate it. We will fret
when we should feast because we fear we lack the means to overcome,
not remembering that in Christ we already have overcome.

We often confine our concept of victory to not losing, not looking
foolish, or not falling behind. We might think of victory as dodging
danger, bringing order to chaos, or outsmarting the enemy. But victory for the Christian is endurance, relinquishing control, loving the
enemy. It is gained by not going outside of God's will to get it. There's
no such thing as winning at the expense of God's glory.

Instead, we are nourished by Christ to overcome evil with good,
to wage war differently than the world does (2 Corinthians 10:3), and
not to misplace our trust (Psalm 20:7; 146:3; Job 31:24). Scripture
tells us about our God-given weapons and how to use them (Romans
12:21; 2 Corinthians 6:7; 10:3-5; Ephesians 6:10-18; 1 Peter 3:9). God
resources us *toward* peace.

Ephesians 6:12 says, "We wrestle not against flesh and blood, but
against the rulers, against the authorities, against the cosmic powers
over this present darkness, against the spiritual forces of evil in the
heavenly places." When we believe our enemies come only from outside, we leave ourselves vulnerable. We misdiagnose the greatest dangers to our soul and witness. We are just as susceptible to defeat by
selfishness, pride, pettiness, or greed as we are from the schemes of
our foes.

It's not as though God doesn't care about our human enemies. He
said he will be against those who are against us. Vengeance is his; he

will repay. But in the daily Christian walk, victory has far less to do with the immediate visible demise of our opposition. The dark forces in the spiritual realm that are against us will see defeat. In the meantime, we battle the temptation to brandish enemy arms or adopt their strategy for our fight.

Misunderstanding our real enemies keeps us from celebrating our real victories—like when we don't give in to our worst impulses, when we love those who curse us, or when we suffer for doing good. As it stands, we don't think to ourselves, *My cup runneth over*, when obedience comes at personal cost and we obey anyway. We don't recognize that when we do these things, we've dodged the arrows of death to eat from the table of life. When we overcome evil by good, we toast to the cross that enables our victory in Christ.

TRUST

We do not triumph *through* trust in God, triumph *is* trust in God. The battle is over our trust. My trust is only ever misplaced when it isn't in him. Before we get to the table, we must first respond to the invitation to come near. We subvert an enemy ambush by sheltering in God. We turn our backs on the enemy to turn our gaze toward him in the heat of battle. That requires trust.

Trust means the enemy doesn't launch you into a tailspin of idle worry or frenzied self-defense whenever he appears. But even when once shadowy dangers materialize, the psalmist can divert his full attention to enjoying the Lord's provision and presence at his table. The declaration "My cup overflows" nearly mirrors "I shall not want" but takes it a step further. Instead of simply having enough, the psalmist experiences abundance. Here, God says, "Let me pamper you with peace," while your enemy watches.

Every moment of temptation and spiritual warfare, God invites us to a victory feast. The Lord does not come late to our battles. Early he comes and prepares for our arrival. On our own, we may not be able to find the greenest pasture, survive the darkest valley, or defend against the fiercest of foes, but we belong to one whose goodness and mercy are unrelenting.

In the day to day, the victory we most crave now is victory over our flesh rather than over external enemies, knowing that Christ will defend his own. One day, he will mete out punishment as he sees fit and bring justice whether we see it or not. We may ask now, "Why do the wicked prosper?" But is prosperity sitting unbothered in sin, being lulled deeper into its grasp? The Lord has spread before us everything we need, before every enemy that would wage war against us, "Every child of God defeats this evil world, and we achieve this victory through our faith" (1 John 5:4 NLT).

Taking Our Seat at His Table

Amid every battle we face, God invites us to sit within his refuge. He longs to nourish and encourage us. He wants us to trust that he's given us himself—precisely what we need to overcome. Just as sure as the cross is behind us, victory lies before us because our lives are hidden in the Victor's. The sin we've long struggled with won't always get the best of us. We aren't doomed to repeated failure. We can rest knowing the Lord's presence transcends what we feel. Just like the flow of the air, he is moving even if his movements cannot be perceived. And where God is not just felt but known, faith and confidence grow. Affliction is a swindler, so we must guard resolutely our conviction that God is present and that in Christ we overcome.

An old friend used to say, "If you want more grace, be more humble." God is not for the proud. He does not stand on their side. Victory is out of their grasp. God opposes the proud but gives grace to the humble (James 4:6). The proud boast, "I have provided for myself, I can protect myself, and I can win on my own." These do not sit at God's table, nor are they nourished by grace.

See what comforts and assurances lay before you at the Lord's banquet table? Is any other table so secure? Your battles are never too small to escape his notice. The same attentiveness God had with Israel, he had with the psalmist and he has with you. While you may face enemies and hostility, you never do so alone. God is with you. He shelters and protects you. Even under siege, he comes with refreshment. He sets a table before you to transform your panic into peace. He declares his victory with a meal, with oil that refreshes, wine that cheers, and his presence, which settles your soul. This feast is ever available to us. God sets his table always before us in the presence of our enemies. And we who are in Christ gain victory through him. He is Lord of hosts and King of glory, strong and mighty, the Lord, mighty in battle is he. Those who trust in him are secure.

LITURGY FOR VICTORY

Undefeatable King,
I shelter in you.
Thank you for opening my plight to the promise of triumph,
my eyes to the example of triumph,
my soul to the security of triumph.
You are my battle cry.

Lord of Hosts, you command legions of heavenly armies,
and yet you, Lord Near, flex your might before my foes.
Behind me, before me, above me, beside me,
no danger is closer than you.

A table well set is hope for the hunted,
your festal refreshment is my relief.
I drink from your fountains of solace
as you lead me to cruciform victory.

Though countless battles rage, my heart can rest.
At your table, you calm my thoughts.

Please steady me, Lord, lest I should rush
to battle on my own.

In you, I have victory.
In you, I overcome.
To the cornered, your table is peace.
Better a feast than unauthorized arms
to try to dodge defeat.

Preserve me from every threat.
From the threat of fear
of unsanctioned battle
of repaying evil for evil
or of joyless resignation.

Grant that I might live in your victory
over my enemies,
over my sin,
over death.

Amen.

Chapter 5

FEAST OF THE TRANSFORMED WILDERNESS

To the Thirsty

My soul will be satisfied as with fat and rich food,
and my mouth will praise you with joyful lips.

PSALM 63:5

If ever a soul was thirsty, it was mine.

I'd spent three years circling the dry and weary desert of God's absence with no end in sight. Two and a half years in, an old friend came to visit and asked how I was doing. I thought I'd gotten away with the perfunctory "fine" until my housemate told her to ask me again. When she did, I broke down in the most soul-scraping tears I've ever cried. For several hours, all I could get out through the sobs was, "What else am I supposed to do?" I'd tried all I'd known to reclaim something of the intimacy I'd once enjoyed with God. Yet after three dispiriting years, his absence still bore brutally down on my soul. I wrote in my journal, "Why do you watch as I'm crushed by the unbearable weight of your continued absence? Why do you continue to give me life without giving me yourself?"

DESIRE

Raw, unmet desire sits at the heart of Psalm 63. The fellowship the psalmist once enjoyed with God has been interrupted, and his thirst for him has reached critical levels. Derek Kidner observes, "The longing of these verses is not the groping of a stranger, feeling his way towards God, but the eagerness of a friend, almost of a lover, to be in touch with the one he holds dear."[1] The deeper the relationship, the more deeply felt the loss, and the more desperate the search. We see it in its opening lines, "My soul thirsts for you, my flesh faints for you, as in a dry and weary land where there is no water" (Psalm 63:1). No cool love for God could have produced this thirst. Only a being sustained by water notices its absence. The same goes for a soul once sustained by God.

The wilderness of Judea provides the backdrop to this psalm. The desert's leeward mountains blocked the rain and wind coming from Jerusalem. For most, the wilderness was a thoroughfare, not a destination. It was a place for wandering, fleeing, and hiding. Whether David, the psalmist, was on the run from Saul's jealousy (1 Samuel 18:6-20) or his son Absalom's betrayal and thirst for power (2 Samuel 15–19), this much was clear: the psalmist's soulscape mirrored his landscape. When he compares his soul with "a dry and weary land where there is no water,"[2] he's not comparing it with something he's never experienced, but with the harsh and unforgiving desert he'd come to know all too well.

The psalmist measures the distance he feels from God in thirst, drawing on his immediate surroundings to capture just how parched he is. But parched he does not remain. The rest of the psalm unpacks how his inner wilderness is transformed into a feast through a fixed gaze, staid mind, reprioritized life, and adhered soul. He reveals what propels him to praise. While this psalm isn't intended as a manual for renewed intimacy with God, it does portray the psalmist's journey to finding the fullness and joy of the Lord in the wilderness. It can stretch our holy imagination for what God can do even amidst dry times and for what he invites us to in every wilderness season.

THE IMPACT OF ABSENCE

Both Psalm 23 from the last chapter and this psalm are psalms of confidence, but their differences are stark. In Psalm 23, God drives most of the action; in Psalm 63, the psalmist appears to. He seeks, he enjoys, he feasts, he clings, and he rejoices. Yet implicit even in these actions is something of a testimony about God. Psalm 23 begins with abundance and green pastures but darkens in the middle with valleys and foes. Psalm 63 begins dark with the fainthearted and ends with struggle, but lightens in the middle, bursting with praise.

The psalmist's circumstances in Psalm 63 seem static: he stays in the desert throughout and is only transported away by thinking about the Lord. By contrast, in Psalm 23, the psalmist changes settings at least five times—from pasturelands, to waters, valleys, battlefields, and the house of the Lord—with God stuck to his side. God's presence is stressed in Psalm 23, his absence in Psalm 63. But despite the "not yet" tension of Psalm 63, it is filled with more praise and bolder claims of God's goodness than when the psalmist experiences God's continual presence in Psalm 23.

Whether it's the sheep in green pastures, the assaulted at his table, or the thirsty in the wilderness, in both psalms we see God feeding us. Whether God feels present or distant, he feeds us. Whether we're on the move or stuck in place, he feeds us. And whether we're gaining victory on battlefields or fainting in deserts, he feeds us.

EARLY SOUGHT

The psalm opens with a declaration of devotion: "O God, you are my God." The Hebrew emphasizes the psalmist's sole allegiance to God. God alone he trusts. Given his circumstances, myriad other things could have been his god, but he did not resort to either idol-making, grumbling—a fatalistic and faithless airing of needs—self-reliance, or worry in the wilderness. Rather, his words affirmed the first commandment: he would have no gods before God. None in reserve for difficult days. No golden calf, no graven image, nor the comforts of palace life. And, as we will see, not even survival itself. He neither fills his soul with inferior goods nor pretends his thirst isn't there. Instead, the psalmist single-mindedly pursues God and desires him above all else.

Before we're even fully introduced to the conflict within this psalm, the psalmist describes his relief efforts: "Earnestly I seek you." The Hebrew verb translated "earnestly seek" comes from a noun meaning dawn or daybreak. The implication is that one seeks early what is most important. The break of day found the psalmist's whole being outstretched in search of God. His affections, intellect, memory, desires, will, faculties, and very body itself were given over to that search. The psalmist's precarious situation in the desert was, perhaps unexpectedly, not his central concern. Rather, the precarious condition of his soul absorbed him. As he triaged the wilderness, seeking God came first, both in his soul and in his day.

Sometimes it's hard to tell the difference between hunger and thirst, as symptoms of dehydration and hunger overlap. We recognize a feeling of emptiness, but we reach for the wrong thing to fill it. Similarly, sometimes we can misdiagnose the root of our listlessness, loneliness, weariness, pain, or shadowed spirit. We reach for changed circumstances, not realizing that only God's presence can provide what we truly need. But the psalmist saw the vacancy in his soul correctly, and while he knew he couldn't force God's presence, that couldn't stop him from seeking his Lord.

DISSATISFIED SOUL AND FLESH

To speak of one's soul, *nephesh* in Hebrew, was to speak of one's whole self. While Western thought divides the self into body and soul, *nephesh* was the whole being, complete with its desires and longings.[3] It derived from the word that originally meant throat and expressed physical needs like hunger and thirst. *Nephesh* here portrays the psalmist's thirsting after God "as a fundamental appetite of the worshipper."[4] Psalm 42 also uses imagery of a soul that thirsts and pants after God (Psalm 42:1-2), but there it goes unresolved. His fainting flesh paralleled his thirsty soul and emphasized his deep desire for God (Psalm 63:1-2).

It wasn't as though he couldn't have had other desires. In contrast with the "I shall not want" of Psalm 23, the displaced psalmist in Psalm 63 could have produced a long list of wants. Several times in the account of his fleeing from Absalom, Scripture mentions that David grew weary in his wandering and faced uncertainty (2 Samuel 16:14; 17:2, 29). But, despite having much to complain about or desire—his son's betrayal, homesickness, scarce resources, and plentiful opposition—he didn't recount all he'd lost. His sole expressed need was for God.

Elsewhere in the psalms, we find examples aplenty, less joyful and more pained, of the psalmist detailing worldly hardships. But his mind isn't fixed on those things here. In this psalm, his supreme hardship is spiritual: the distance from God he experiences. God welcomes, even requires, us to bring him our troubles. He wants us to come to him with our needs and what ails us. The psalmist does precisely that: what he recognizes he most needs is God and what ails him most is God's absence. What felt most acute—that stung worse than betrayal, that weakened more than constant enemy pursuit, and that wearied more than the parched earth—was the exhaustion of his soul. He had scoured the wilderness for the nourishment that was God himself alone. What he craved was the company of his God.

BEHELD POWER AND GLORY

But the psalmist does not wallow in his thirst. The first balm he sought for his weary soul was a tired glance at the sanctuary. His seeking did not first bring him to look for escape, but to try to collapse the distance between himself and his God. At that time, God was thought to have a specific dwelling place. Though God had broad jurisdiction and controlled everything everywhere, he had a home address and could be visited in one place: the sanctuary housing the ark of the covenant. That, however, was located in Jerusalem, not the wilderness, so when the psalmist says he has looked upon God in the sanctuary, he's drawing on his past experience. He will seek God wherever he can.

This Hebrew verb for "looked upon" suggests *to contemplate with pleasure*. The psalmist first contemplates God's character: the power and glory seen in his sanctuary. God's utility did not precede his majesty. He was fascinated by who God was, the mere thought of him sent his hands up in worship. He didn't soothe his ache with the things of the world but delighted himself in God's power and glory.

In the wilderness, when we fix our eyes on who God is, he can quench our thirst. Fixation on anything else will leave us wanting. Often, the reason our hearts are not drawn to God's glory is because they are pulled elsewhere. They are otherwise enchanted. The heart has not been filled and fed by God, but instead by the world and its many fleeting attractions. Once it has gone and had its fill of the profane, no space remains for the divine. Perhaps the thought of God's power and glory just doesn't sound appealing. Out of a sea of contenders for our attention and affection, God just barely makes the list. No sooner than I say I will sit down to attend to my soul, do I end up attending to countless trivial diversions instead. I can stand to be entertained for much longer than I can to be spiritually fed. Our attention span for holy things is critically short.

For the psalmist to say he thirsts indicates he desires God even while confessing there's a deep emptiness inside he hoped God would fill but hasn't. His thirst is a sign of his desire. It's a pulse showing that he's still spiritually alive. "God, I desire more of you than I'm experiencing," "God, I want to want more of you," and "God, I confess I don't desire you," are all healthy confessions. They betray traces of grace. To varying degrees, they all acknowledge God is personal, pleasurable, and able to satisfy, and that we know intimacy, joy, and fullness in him are a part of our life in him. The danger is when we desire everything before God and don't even know it; when our receptors to the God ache within us no longer function.

Only those whose souls are oriented toward God can be fully satisfied by him. The love of God cannot fully penetrate the heart with no appetite for it, just as savory foods cannot satisfy cravings for something sweet. The heart unaffected by God's power and glory, that has not even the faintest craving for him, is like those broken cisterns that can hold no water (Jeremiah 2:13). Those who find him and his power and glory small and unimpressive will leak joy and contentment and will never be filled. God's love will never satisfy. However, "the believer, by fresh displays of divine glory, is disenchanted from the fascination of the world"[5] and can only be filled by God.

A Love Better Than Life

After looking upon God in his sanctuary, the psalmist makes one of the boldest claims of the entire psalter: "Because your steadfast love is better than life, my lips will praise you" (Psalm 63:3). What love is this which eclipses life itself?

Steadfast love, or in Hebrew *hesed*, is the same word translated "mercy" in Psalm 23—"Goodness and mercy shall follow me." While God's glory and power could be seen apart from his dealings with mankind, nature itself bearing witness to these attributes, *hesed* was the way of God with his people. It was a mystery of cosmic proportions that one so transcendent would choose as he chose, bear as he bore, and deliver as he delivered. He suffers long, woos tenderly, and yearns for our nearness more than we his.

There are many ways to translate this word: "great love" (NIV), "steadfast love" (ESV), "mercies" (KJV), "kindness" (CEV), "faithful love" (HCSB). However it's translated, *hesed* is intensely relational. It's the most devoted, ardent, unfailing love that exists. Of its 248 occurrences in the Bible, most are in the psalms, and appear frequently together with *faithfulness, covenant,* and *tender mercies. Hesed* is covenantal, faultlessly loyal, patient, and fulfilling. It extends to the heavens, fills the earth, and is from everlasting to everlasting. Because of this loyal love, God notices, remembers, redeems, and restores his people. Though the psalmist might grow weary, *hesed* would endure and follow him into eternity, even if he met his end in the desert. Neither desert nor distance will outlast God's loving-kindness. This is the steadfast love the psalmist says is better than life. It is his treasure, his pearl of great price.

A REPRIORITIZED LIFE

The psalmist says God's steadfast love is better than life. Better than his material possessions, comfort, prestige and honor, and all the fleeting and fickle trappings of life. For modern people that may include a high-paying job; a significant other or spouse; political stability and power; family; freedom; being attractive, smart, or successful; reputation; status quo; savings account; cheap thrills; credentials; being well-known or well-liked; social media follower count and influence; connections; health; material possessions; and whatever else you may desire or value. His love is more to be sought, more to be valued, and more to be enjoyed. For his better-than-life love warms the shadowed heart, declutters the anxious mind, and buoys the sunken soul. By design there are depths from which only it can retrieve us and heights to which only it can propel us. Hugh Black writes,

We were born for the love of God; if we do not find it, it were better for us if we had never been born. We may have tasted of all the joys the world can offer, have known success and the gains of success, been blessed with the sweetest friendships and the fiercest loves; but if we have not found this chief end of life, we have missed our chance, and can only have at the last a desolated life.[6]

A Feasted Soul

In light of all the psalmist has seen in the sanctuary and a love that puts all of life in its proper perspective, his soul feasts. The psalmist's insides no longer match his surroundings. The wilderness within has transformed.

Fat and rich foods are not the foods of hunger, thirst, or subsistence. They are the food of pleasure. Likewise, God's power, glory, and steadfast love are meant to please us as well. The Hebrew word here translated fat or marrow, *heleb*—or the fat cut from the slaughtered animal pre-sacrifice—came to mean the choicest part of something. When Pharaoh tells Joseph he will eat of the fat of the land (Genesis 45:18), this is what he means. Eating this part of an animal, however, was prohibited precisely because it was the richest part, and therefore belonged to God (Leviticus 3:16-17; 7:23-27). This fat, translated as rich food, became a figurative stand-in for abundance. "God's love has been laid before him as a feast of the 'richest of foods'...reserved only for God but laid on the banquet table of the psalmist's life."[7] God does not primarily want to be used, especially for mere survival. Instead, he wants to be supremely enjoyed. The psalmist doesn't say here that he enjoys God as bread, a staple food, but as fat, a delicacy. The choice of menu is deliberate. He wants to be experienced as the choicest and most fulfilling of all we consume. When he is experienced this way, the worries and cares surrounding us recede and a feast comes to the fore.

LATE REMEMBERED

Finally, when the terrors of beast and enemy descend at night, once again, the psalmist fills his mind with God. The psalm opened with the declaration that the psalmist sought the Lord early, and now he also seeks him late: "I remember you upon my bed, and meditate on you in the watches of the night" (Psalm 63:6). These watches recurred every few hours until sunrise. It's not that God bookends David's day, but that he permeates it. From daybreak *through* sunrise—the whole day and night—the psalmist has God on his mind. At any time of the day, you could find his thoughts full of him. How foreign to most of us! In the context of our anxieties, we understand that what keeps us awake at night remains in our minds throughout the day. But not in the context of our God. Preston suggests, "Why not collect our affections, and gather up our scattered thoughts, which are busy with a thousand trifles, and bestow them all on him who is the fullness of all excellence, beauty, and perfection?"[8] Too often, we know little of this single-mindedness when it comes to God.

Interspersed between his seeking, feasting, and remembering, the psalmist is filled with praise. His lips praise God (verse 3), he blesses God and lifts his hands in his name (verse 4), his mouth praises God with joyful lips (verse 5), and he sings for joy in the shadow of his wings (verse 7). Praise seems to spill forth from his every effort to seek after God, for "those who seek him shall praise his name" (Psalm 22:26). These are the actions of someone who has found a portal in the wilderness that leads to a feast.

A STEADFAST MIND

Only when the psalmist remembers and meditates on who God is can he begin to fill himself at the feast. God was the interceptor of his despair-bound thoughts. He kept him safe and was his relief in times of distress. He was the sustainer and upholder of his life, and the psalmist found his ultimate satisfaction in him.

God was everything to him and to be without him was to have nothing: to not be able to find his way, to fumble in the dark, to be tired, defenseless, and disrobed. Apart from him, all was a chasing after the wind and a grasping after a life never to be found. Even if his enemy were to be defeated and he left the wilderness behind, all would be for naught if God did not slake his thirst.

This psalm is a defiant declaration of *yet*. "Though I thirst, *yet* I will seek you," "*Yet* I will set my soul to reconstructing your excellencies and praising, delighting in, and remembering you," and "*Yet* I will feed on and savor you in this dry and weary land." The same contentment our bodies feel after finishing an incredible meal, our souls can feel after beholding and remembering God. With God, the psalmist is able to feast in the wilderness.

Wilderness Seasons

One thing I wish I'd known in the midst of my first desert was that we will all go through seasons—often through no fault of our own. Even David, a man after God's own heart, felt far from him at times. In the early days, I'd been encouraged to do more—more Bible reading, more prayer, more trusting. And yet, three years in, round and round the desert I went, spiritual disciplines in hand. To travel the wilderness thinking there's a formula to its escape is to heap heartache on top of the thirst. Let us resist that temptation. Sometimes God parks us in wildernesses for reasons we don't—and may never—know, but we can always trust he can and does feed us there.

Tucked away and simply stated near the end of the psalm is a beautiful and comforting admission that despite God's felt absence, the psalmist knows he's being upheld. God *is* there. It's the only place in the whole psalm where God is the subject, instead of the psalmist. In verse 8 he says, "My soul clings to you, your right hand upholds me." Because he is upheld he can cling, however tight or tired his grip. God's hand lifts the psalmist to his throne and sustains his search. My exasperated tears at three years of God's absence were only possible because God's right hand held me fast. When I finally reached the end of myself, I realized that even my desire for him was given by grace. I wrote again in my journal,

> I have come to see I cannot produce desire for God. I have watched myself be stripped of all those spiritual things I had taken pride in and am out of all options. But though I did not have what it took to run after him, he came and found me in my pit with nothing to offer him and reminded me, "This is how you come, broken and empty-handed, not put together."

What We Seek

We all seek something and could benefit from reflecting on what that is. One year for Lent, I gave up daydreaming. Every time a desire popped into my head for something I didn't have, I wrote it down. At the end of the day, I prayed through the list in my notebook, asking the Lord to show me how he wanted to meet those needs. Mark Futato states,

> In the wilderness we find ourselves on a search. A search for answers, for security, for meaning, for significance. Yes, on the surface we may be searching for these or similar things. But in our souls we are on a search that only God himself can satisfy by his own presence. Psalm 63 was given to guide us in that search and to lead us to an experience of deep satisfaction.[9]

The psalm ends and David has no idea when or if his situation will change. But he's learned satisfaction in the desert. The superscript says he wrote this psalm in the wilderness, not after he'd left it. Paul makes a similar statement in Philippians when he says he knows how to abound, how to be brought low, and how to be content in all circumstances, including in hunger and in need (Philippians 4:11-12). God loves to be sought and the psalmist recognizes that even though he's dry, God has been his help (Psalm 63:7) and God's right hand holds him fast (verse 8).

The people of God are God-seekers wherever we find ourselves, regardless of the hour, the season, or circumstance. And fortunately for us, God loves to reveal himself to us. What we learn from his perceived absences is powerful and purposeful. Contrary to what we may think, those wilderness seasons are not meant to starve us. In our reaching and grasping after God, they are meant to feed us in ways we've never been fed. In them, we can feast on the fat and rich food that the psalmist does. Our journey to God's table may be different, but God shows us through this psalm that feasting is possible.

WE FEAST

So rarely are our days as saturated with thoughts of God as the psalmist's. He does not make one reference to God's utility, but to God's superiority over his current and even his desired circumstances. Even if life itself were to slip away, should God's love be grasped, he would erupt with praise. This is not faking fine, or sweeping pain under the rug, but holding to the truth of what God's love for us has accomplished in and for us. We do all that we can to hang on to life. And life is precious indeed. But there is something more precious still.

In the midst of my season of extended unemployment where I sometimes was unable to provide for myself, had lost a close friend, and had injured myself but couldn't afford treatment, I remember writing to a friend about what that season had taught me: "Having experienced both now, I can say unequivocally that it is bitter beyond comparison to have all that you want but to grasp for the Lord and not feel his presence than to rebound from heartache to heartache experiencing him at your side." After each setback, I felt like a struck bop bag slowly returning upright. But instead of being worked on by the forces of gravity, I was worked on by the force of God's love that set me over and over again back on my feet.

We ought to pray for ourselves each day, whether in the wilderness or gardens, for the power to understand the length, width, height, and depth of the love of Christ, that we may be filled to the measure of all the fullness of God (Ephesians 3:19). To this suite of descriptors the psalmist adds how thirst-quenching and pleasing and supreme is the love of God. Not only does it fill our most basic needs, but our highest desires. Because of this, the psalmist says that his soul was satisfied as with the choicest of food. It was satisfied as with God himself, fully convinced of God's love. As Samuel Rutherford writes:

> Convene all your lovers before your soul, and give them
> their leave; and strike hands with Christ, that thereafter
> there may be no happiness to you but Christ, no hunt-
> ing for anything but Christ, no bed at night, when death
> cometh, but Christ. Christ, Christ, who but Christ!...All
> lovers blush when ye stand beside Christ![10]

The satiated soul's first language is praise. We do not praise our way out of the wilderness; rather, we praise our way into an unshakeable preoccupation with God's promise-keeping kindness that overpowers our preoccupation with the barrenness around us. Our lips are too busy extolling his excellencies, our souls too flooded with recollections of his grace, and our hands too tightly clutching his promises to surrender to our circumstances. The wilderness remains the same, but we are changed, and because we are changed, the wilderness is transformed, too, into a feast. And we therefore do not despair when he feels far off; even as he upholds us. God can use these means of grace to turn our deserts into feasts—one morsel of his goodness, power, and glory at a time.

LITURGY FOR REFRESHMENT

Water of Life,
would you meet me here where all I feel is abandoned?
Help me to know your presence in your absence,
the indelible trace of your Spirit on my desires,
though unperceived by my other senses.
I have no other streams but yours.

Refresh me, O God, and set a table in my soul
where I can be, and cry, and grasp as I wait.
Though my heart hurts from hope,
and my eyes are weak from squinting,
I have saved you a seat and bid you come.

Nourish me, O God, bring me back to life;
may your creation remind me you're near.
Surround me with those who'll fetch water for me
when I can't find my way on my own.

It is heavy, your absence, it sits on my chest.
Father, would you bring relief,
restore the joy of your companionship.
But if not, please carry me still.

Chapter 6

WISDOM THROWS A FEAST

To the Fool

Wisdom has built her house; she has hewn her seven pillars. She has slaughtered her beasts; she has mixed her wine; she has also set her table. She has sent out her young women to call from the highest places in the town, "Whoever is simple, let him turn in here!" To him who lacks sense she says, "Come, eat of my bread and drink of the wine I have mixed. Leave your simple ways, and live, and walk in the way of insight."

PROVERBS 9:1-6

Atop the heights of a city in a palatial home furnished with treasures from all corners and every age of the earth, Lady Wisdom tends to her guests and gets ready for more. Hers is a feast without beginning or end. Fanning out like a search party, her messengers call out on her behalf to simple and senseless passersby, "Whoever is simple, let him turn in here!" (Proverbs 9:4).

Foot traffic begins to split: the majority turn away, continuing on their way—a band of scoffers who believe themselves already wise

(Proverbs 26:12). But the ears of those who know they are simple perk up at the invitation. Their pace quickens in her direction, an unfamiliar but inviting aroma intensifying with each stride. Spiced wine? Fatty meat? The warm bread of Wisdom? With sumptuous and exotic fare, no menu compared with hers. A chance to dine with the daily delight of the divine (Proverbs 8:30)? None was more desirable than she (Proverbs 3:15; 8:11).

As a young girl, Wisdom danced about the cosmic stage of creation as the heavens and earth took shape (Proverbs 8:22-31). As she matured, she bewitched and bewildered many with her incisive yet veiled wit. Over shared food and drink she revealed her secrets; the longer you stayed, the more she would divulge. She had an otherworldly radiance about her. In the noncanonical book of Wisdom a suitor once praised, "Hers is a brightness that never grows dim, and I preferred it to any other light."[1] She was the kind of companion who changed you.

The grandeur of Wisdom's home varied based on who you asked. Should a fool peek through her gates, they'd be unimpressed by what appeared to them to be a decrepit shack cramped with tawdry trinkets and fools. But to the simpleton who entered her doors, its rooms appeared spacious, its construction sturdy, its contents refined, and the conviviality within infectious.

This feast was no potluck; Lady Wisdom did all the work. As a host, Lady Wisdom left no detail unconsidered. She didn't fear running out of food or space at her table. Wisdom's spread included staples such as understanding and knowledge. But also on her table were the unexpected delicacies of rebuke and discipline.

Aside from her impressive menu, her gatherings brought together the best of company, amiable yet unassuming. Wisdom insisted they come empty-handed and ready to receive. She embraced everyone at her door, honoring each guest with crowns of splendor and garlands of grace (Proverbs 3:35; 4:8).

It's staggering that a woman of Wisdom's status would deign to invite the simple-minded and the common. Prior to their entry, however else they differed, they shared an awareness of their need. Guests content to just pop in left with grumbling stomachs. But dish after dish, morsel after morsel, cup after cup, those who lingered were filled with goodness and a growing appetite for Life.

How anyone reached the city's summit was itself a wonder. No road was as beset with obstacles as the one leading up to Lady Wisdom's home. From the entrance to her house, you could see the road behind dotted with traps and dead ends. Gangs who loved to chase evil lay in wait for blood and ambushed the innocent without reason (Proverbs 1:11), preying on the weak and vulnerable. Aimless wanderers devised and rejoiced in wicked schemes (Proverbs 2:12-15).

The journey was harrowing, but the reward well worth it. Her rooftop view was spectacular, as the pockets of danger disappeared with elevation. Over the hum of revelers below, you could hear the flickering flames of the rooftop altar and inhale their earthy mixed notes of cassia, cinnamon, and saffron as the flames stretched and strained toward heaven in worship.

FEASTING ON WISDOM

In Proverbs 9, God uses the imagery of a feast to illustrate the pursuit and acquisition of wisdom. Be it a wedding reception, holiday, birthday, or another notable event, feasting is universal. While details and motivations may vary, everyone knows that feeling of coming away full, of being surrounded by excellent company, and the near-delirium of time so well spent that worry turns to mist.

When it comes to wisdom, do a similar set of images spring to mind? Do we envision a feast—piling high our plates, going back for seconds, bonding with friends new and old, and getting caught up in a flurry of boisterous joy? If you're at all like me, that thought probably never came to mind.

Yet here we are—presented in Scripture with an open invitation, a larger-than-life venue, an enticing and generous host, exceptional food and company, all designed to make the pursuit of wisdom a bigger deal than a boxed lunch eaten at your desk. More often than not, though, we merely nibble at Wisdom's feast. We pop in, we're picky eaters, or we RSVP "no" and barge ahead in our own understanding.

DEFINING WISDOM

King Solomon wrote Proverbs to his young son. Father-son address was a typical format for ancient wisdom literature. The first nine chapters of the book alternate between paternal appeals to pursue wisdom and Lady Wisdom's appeal on her own behalf. Solomon states several reasons for writing: that his son might know and understand wisdom, that his new grasp of that wisdom would make him righteous and just, and that he might exercise prudence (Proverbs 1:2-4). But among these goals he has another. Proverbs 24:13-14 says, "My son, eat honey, for it is good, and the drippings of the honeycomb are sweet to your taste. Know that wisdom is such to your soul." He wants his son to understand that wisdom is not just foundational, but sweet.

What is wisdom? Is it more than the art of living well? More than the ability to navigate gray areas or read people or choose between two good options? The Hebrew word for wisdom, *hokma,* implies "mastery over experience through the intellectual, emotional, and spiritual state of knowing."[2] Throughout Proverbs, wisdom is not just intellectual, but also ethical and theological. Intellectually, it relies on knowledge; it is truth-oriented. Ethically, it is used in the service of justice, equity, and righteousness; it is action-oriented. Theologically, God is wisdom's sole source and the fear of God is identified as wisdom's beginning; it is worship-oriented. Wisdom is multifaceted.

Wisdom includes what you know, how you live, and who or what you worship. Wisdom gives us the insight and knowledge we need to live upright, just, and unbiased lives out of reverence for God that profit our neighbor. It allows us to be as "shrewd as serpents" yet "innocent as doves" (Matthew 10:16). It enables us to do God's work in God's ways for God's glory. It teaches us how to wound to heal, how to die to live, and how to reenact the care of the Creator. Wisdom deftly handles knotty situations, big decisions, and complicated interpersonal relationships, all with an ear to heaven.

The rich imagery used to describe wisdom in Scripture has implications for how we approach it. The festal setting makes clear that God is not simply utilitarian in dispensing wisdom, but lavish. Can we imagine ourselves eating at Wisdom's table? Will we indulge ourselves in the Bible, communion with the Spirit, piling high counsel from wise companions? How might we feast on the knowledge, understanding, discipline, instruction, and rebuke on Wisdom's table?

KNOWLEDGE

Knowledge, like wisdom, springs from the fear of the Lord (Proverbs 1:7; 2:5). Like understanding, it also brings pleasure (Proverbs 2:10). Although it is a general term, the Hebrew word for knowledge often implies knowledge of someone. In Proverbs, especially, the object of knowledge is frequently God.

God's Word and creation both contain knowledge. In Psalm 119, the psalmist seeks knowledge in the commands of God (verse 66). In Psalm 19, nature reveals the knowledge of God; by its testimony, we see God's power and divinity (Romans 1:20). Memories make some of the best sources of knowledge: the memories of the people of God as recorded in the Bible and the personal stories of God's character made manifest in the pages of our lives. Both God's Word and his world teach us.

Knowledge can be kept in reserves. The wise store up knowledge (Proverbs 10:14) but fools hate it (Proverbs 1:22); they never have enough when they need it. When God warns Israel about being exiled from the land he'd given them, he places the blame for such a drastic consequence on their lack of knowledge (Isaiah 5:13). By contrast, knowledge delivers the righteous (Proverbs 11:9). To have knowledge in abundance is wise, to lack it proves a liability.

UNDERSTANDING

Translations of the Hebrew word for understanding vary between *understanding, discerning, consider,* and *perceive.* To understand is to be attuned to the subtleties of application. Understanding is processed knowledge; it's what we make of what we know after sitting and wrestling with it. When learning a foreign language, you might know all the vocabulary and grammar from class but not be fully able to understand. Understanding often comes from frequent use in a variety of real-world settings where you learn not just when to use the right word, but how the locals would use it, as well as how to read the nonverbal clues operative in that particular culture.

Those who understand have a taste for wisdom. "On the lips of him who has understanding, wisdom is found" (Proverbs 10:13) and "Wisdom is pleasure to a man of understanding" (Proverbs 10:23).

One way to feast on understanding would be to learn from others' experiences. I recently watched a television show about a virtual reality game where you could form alliances with other players and by doing so gain their experience points. We can learn from older or younger believers, or from peers who come from different backgrounds. We can learn from Christ followers in the Global South. For these we must learn to listen well. Then we can desire more than mere entertainment or shared interests from our friendships—we can be interested in how our friends have been formed. For this, we need curiosity and transparency. Even from those with whom we clash we can learn, provided we have the maturity and willingness to see their strengths. In addition to being willing to listen to others' experiences, we must be willing to share our own. Understanding also helps the wise absorb rebuke, as Proverbs 17:10 says, "A rebuke goes deeper into a man of understanding than a hundred blows into a fool."

REBUKE

When I lived in China, I once attended a traditional countryside wedding. At the reception, a server set a plate of jiggly, semi translucent cubes on the lazy Susan at the center of my table. Confused and suspicious, I asked what it was and if and how to eat it (I had once confused tripe for moist towelettes and wiped my hands with it to everyone's horror). The gelatinous substance was pure fat. My shock and discomfort registered on my face and the entire table erupted in laughter, joking about how Americans couldn't imagine a plate of fat—with no meat—as a delicacy. They weren't wrong. Where I was from animal fat was discarded, not eaten, and *definitely* not dignified. This, I imagine, is what a simpleton's first encounter with rebuke on Wisdom's table might have been like.

To the world outside Wisdom's doors, rebuke is a shameful slight. But at her feast, it is a delicacy to be savored. Augustine wrote, "Who else causes a rebuke to be salutary and produces the correction in the heart of the one rebuked in order to bring him to the heavenly kingdom?"[3] At wisdom's feast, rebuke brought honor. "Those who have receptive ears, however, welcome rebuke, even love it (Proverbs 9:8), because they see it for what it is: not a punishment but a guide, not an end in itself but a means to greater wisdom."[4] Again and again, Proverbs links wisdom and rebuke, using one's response to rebuke as a way to distinguish between the wise and the foolish.

Even though we know in our minds that rebuke protects against folly and ruin, can we imagine ourselves giving thanks for it as one of God's good gifts? Loving those who dish it out? Perhaps loving them even more because of it? Can we picture ourselves savoring rebuke—regardless of its presentation—not just because it's nutrient dense but because we find it sweet? Could we prefer it to the slow poison of flattery? Would we ever dream of going back for seconds or thirds?

DISCIPLINE

Discipline is often spoken of as a sign of paternal love and belonging. I'd be unreservedly enthusiastic about it if it didn't hurt so badly. We'd probably all be. Part of growing in wisdom, however, is being able to distinguish between how something feels, its value, and its eventual fruit. Something can make you feel good while killing you. Sometimes painful experiences can be invaluable for bearing fruit. Discipline tutors us. Discipline can be a difficult relationship, rejection, being stuck in a job you dislike, or loss. Discipline offers us opportunities to be stretched, to recalibrate our identity and sense of self-worth, to return our focus on God and reliance on him in facing a desire achingly unmet. The world conditions us to make associations among feelings, value, and eventual fruit where none exist and to miss them when they couldn't be more clear. It tells us that what feels best is best *for* us and anything difficult is bad. There's no need for patient endurance, the way forward is eliminating whatever stretches you or makes you uncomfortable.

Knowing this, Solomon reminds his son: "My son, do not despise the Lord's discipline or be weary of his reproof, for the Lord reproves him whom he loves, as a father the son in whom he delights" (Proverbs 3:11-12). Discipline is desirable because it comes down from loving hands as an expression of his delight. Discipline is one of God's love languages in dealing with us.

Hebrews 12 quotes Proverbs 3 and further develops it, explaining discipline's benefits while openly acknowledging its accompanying pain. Discipline is categorically "for our good" so that we may "share in [God's] holiness" (Hebrews 12:10). It yields the peaceful fruit of righteousness to those who have been trained by it (Hebrews 12:11). The cry of the psalmist captures this sentiment: "It was good for me to be afflicted that I might learn your decrees" (Psalm 119:71 NIV). Knowing its benefits, the wise do not resent discipline while the fool dies for lack of it (Proverbs 5:23). What matters most when hard things happen isn't necessarily our ability to correctly categorize what's discipline and what's just bad luck, but to have a disposition primed and ready to learn and grow when the opportunity presents itself. This disposition prays, "Lord, if there is anything to be learned here, any area for growth that this situation has uncovered, please help me not miss it."

INSTRUCTION

More so than knowledge or understanding, instruction carries with it the idea that someone provided procedures or directions with the expectation we will obey. Knowing that your mom is caring is different than knowing that she wants you to take 1000 mg of Tylenol, make yourself some honey and lemon tea, and get some rest. These are separate things, but they do work together, reinforcing each other. If it wasn't your mother suggesting this, but an enemy or someone whose medical license had been revoked due to malpractice, you'd have cause to be wary of the instructions.

The instructions referred to in the book of Proverbs deal with those same three areas of the book as a whole: the intellectual, the ethical, and the theological. Proverbs counts instruction as essential to living true to what we already know, "Cease to hear instruction, my son, and you will stray from the words of knowledge" (Proverbs 19:27). We progress in wisdom with more instruction, "Give instruction to a wise man, and he will be still wiser; teach a righteous man, and he will increase in learning" (Proverbs 9:9).

Instruction is social, requiring a teacher and a student. But it's also social in the sense that bad or ignored instructions make folly more highly contagious. "Whoever heeds instruction is on the path to life, but he who rejects reproof leads others astray" (Proverbs 10:17).

Finally, an appetite for instruction is a true act of self-love. Proverbs 15:32 says, "Whoever ignores instruction despises himself." The one who cannot bother to be taught, should not expect to grow in wisdom. The unteachable work against themselves.

HUMILITY

I know a thing or two (or maybe more) about being proud. If you're full of yourself, you can't be full of anything else. That's why the first step toward wisdom is humility. Those who seek her can come no other way. Proverbs 11:2 says, "With the humble is wisdom." Calvin wrote,

> From the feeling of our own ignorance, vanity, poverty, infirmity, and—what is more—depravity and corruption, we recognize that the true light of wisdom, sound virtue, full abundance of every good, and purity of righteousness rest in the Lord alone. To this extent we are prompted by our own ills to contemplate the good things of God; and we cannot seriously aspire to him before we begin to become displeased with ourselves.[5]

The pursuit of wisdom can only be practiced in community. We can't be wise in isolation or when we're enmeshed in the wrong crowd. Proverbs 13:20 says: "Whoever walks with the wise becomes wise." Wisdom provides us fellow revelers from whom we learn and impart wisdom, instruction, and rebuke.

Since our company affects our trajectory, we benefit by surrounding ourselves with the wise, who are portrayed in Proverbs as those who:

- accept commands (Proverbs 10:8; 12:15)

- heed discipline (Proverbs 10:17; 13:1; 15:5,31)

- discern right from wrong (Proverbs 14:8; 16:21)

- store up knowledge (Proverbs 10:14; 18:15)

- nourish others with their words (Proverbs 10:11, 21, 31-32; 11:9, 12; 12:18; 15:2, 4, 7)

- practice judicious speech (Proverbs 16:23)

- pursue understanding (Proverbs 10:23)

- win souls (Proverbs 11:30)

- avoid quarreling (Proverbs 20:3)

- are diligent (Proverbs 10:4), humble (Proverbs 11:2), cautious (Proverbs 14:16), teachable (Proverbs 19:25), slow to anger, and able to overlook an offense (Proverbs 19:11)

This is a community under the influence of Wisdom.

What freedom, boldness, and security exist in a wise community! What soil for growth. In such a community, you could engage in conflict peacefully, anticipating in your neighbor an openness to being corrected and an eagerness to learn from their mistakes. And your neighbor finding the same in you. I have a few such relationships like this in my own life, friendships where we speak the truth in love despite our natural inclination to avoid conflict. We listen with patience and grace, and we trust each other's commitment to our relationship and to Christ to know that we gain more from vulnerable and courageous engagement than avoidance or defensiveness.

An Invitation to Relationship

The language of Wisdom's invitation, when placed beside other passages in Proverbs and noncanonical Jewish texts, suggests Wisdom seeks more than just a meal with us. Scholars have noted the strikingly similar language used to describe Lady Wisdom and a wife or mistress. Tremper Longman notes, "One's relationship with Wisdom is described in sexual terms. One obtains life if one embraces this woman and holds her tight. At this point, we must remember that the primary audience of this text is young men, to whom such a metaphor would speak volumes."[6]

"Blessed is the one who finds wisdom" (Proverbs 3:13), "She is a tree of life to those who lay hold of her; those who hold her fast are called blessed" (Proverbs 3:18), "Do not forsake her, and she will keep you; love her, and she will guard you" (Proverbs 4:6)—this language of finding, holding, loving, and not forsaking would have been evocative of a wife to the ancient reader. Both he who finds a wife and he who finds wisdom "receive favor of the Lord" (Proverbs 3:13; 18:22). Wisdom is described as a "sister" (Proverbs 7:4), then a euphemism for bride. In Proverbs 4:8, we're even told to embrace her. While the meaning of the word *embrace* in English can be literal or figurative, Hebrew only uses it in the physical sense. Both wisdom and an excellent wife are "more precious than jewels" (Proverbs 3:15; 31:10). The noncanonical Book of Wisdom makes explicit what Proverbs hints at in an extended confession to her, "Wisdom I loved; I sought her out when I was young and longed to win her for my bride, and I fell in love with her beauty...She would be my counselor in prosperity and my comfort in anxiety and grief...In her friendship is pure delight."[7]

Perhaps we're only content to become wise as long as it doesn't require revealing the ways we're foolish. Or maybe we seek wisdom when riddled with anxiety only to fling her to the side when our circumstances improve. Often, she asks for hard things—for things that imperil our relationships, endanger our jobs, or allow our peers to surpass us. But so often we would rather keep the relationship, make the questionable work choice, or cling white-knuckled to our rung on the social ladder. Then we have to wonder: what is it we really have a taste for? Rather, to love wisdom would mean to be always on the lookout for her, to preference her ways over our own, even when it costs us. It's to seek her with the same focus and intentionality we do our other loves, and when we find her, as scholar Matthew Poole says, "Let her have command of thy heart, and the conduct of thy life."[8]

Wisdom is not just inviting us to eat and mingle. She summons us to a relationship. She seeks us as her lover. This is her endgame: our joyous devotion to her.

Does wisdom captivate you? Does she hold your attention and put you under her spell? Are you enthralled by her beauty? Would you do anything to have her? Among all that can be gained, is she your prize? Would you forsake all else—pride, priorities, counterfeits—to make her yours? Are you intoxicated with her love (Proverbs 5:19)? Or have you been seduced by another? Or will we simply pass her by, or worse yet, dine at her rival's lethal feast?

LADY FOLLY'S FEAST

Lady Wisdom is not the only invitation given in Proverbs 9. The chapter closes with a rival feast.

Lady Folly also sits atop the city heights. Like Lady Wisdom, her invitation goes out to the simple and in the very same words, no less: "Whoever is simple, let him turn in here!" But her feast is a fraud. Confusing the two feasts would have been understandable considering the identical invitations given at the same time from the same place. The gods were traditionally believed to dwell at the high point of a city, so the location of her house opposite Wisdom's establishes Lady Folly as an idol. Her menu offers only stolen water, bread, and whatever fruit people brought, for they eat the fruit of their own ways. Her guests are the unknowingly dead and the doors to her home open up to Sheol, to the chambers of death (Proverbs 7:27).

Lady Folly's home was filled with an unsavory bunch—those who practiced deceitful counsel (Proverbs 12:5), hated discipline (Proverbs

13:18), told secrets and gossiped (Proverbs 20:19), and who rushed to shed blood (Proverbs 1:10-16). Arrogance, a savage lack of self-awareness, expedient corner-cutting, cowardice, dishonesty, quick tongues, and slow ears marked her guests. They were a society of the unlearned. Conversations around her tables were full of flattery and void of rebuke. No one had either a taste for it or would benefit from correction. "Without an innate receptivity to correction, the fool cannot profit from rebuke."[9] Conflict and selfish ambition abounded, while instruction got overlooked. They hid their annoyance and impatience like a peacock hides its train. Their own opinion was paramount. They denied justice to the oppressed and left the needy to their own devices (Jeremiah 5:28). Maddeningly ignorant of their folly, they claimed to be wise.

Even though Lady Folly and Lady Wisdom lived near each other, Proverbs 9 presents a choice: a scene where guests can't have it both ways. Life or death, wisdom or folly? Guests must choose.

CHRIST, THE WISDOM OF GOD

Proverbs does not get the last word on wisdom; Jesus does. With the coming of Christ, our understanding of wisdom deepens. His life, death, and resurrection make plain what Lady Wisdom could only point to: the embodied wisdom of God (1 Corinthians 1:24) in Christ as the exact imprint of God's nature (Hebrews 1:3). Like Wisdom, Christ invites us to his table through a prophetic call to repent and to eat of his bread and wine. Like Wisdom, he rightfully claims to be the way to life. "The prophetic, sapient, and divine components of [Lady Wisdom's] characterization so interpenetrate one another that she emerges as a unique personality whose only peer is Christ."[10]

In his prayer of thanksgiving for the church in Ephesus, Paul asks that God would give them "the Spirit of wisdom and revelation in the knowledge of him" (Ephesians 1:17). It takes wisdom to know Jesus, and it takes knowing Jesus to get wisdom. Faith lies at the heart of each.

Approaching Wisdom

I've long been guilty of praying for wisdom and then opening my eyes to disappointment when I experience no immediate change. I feel all too comfortable at home with the mindset that wisdom is transactional, immediate, and precisely meted out. We must fight against this view and see wisdom instead as relational, progressive, and abundant.

A friend once advised me, when I asked her thoughts on a delicate situation, to simply "stay close to Jesus." These were helpful words. Wisdom comes in our pursuit of Christ. The truth is, the manner and earnestness with which we seek wisdom is the manner and earnestness with which we seek Christ. We pursue wisdom through him.

God plants wisdom, and it grows when we water it. Hebrews 5:14 speaks to its progressive nature: "Solid food is for the mature, for those who have their powers of discernment trained by constant practice to distinguish good from evil."

Wisdom sprouts and grows from our relationship with Christ. However much of it we imagine we may be able to have, God gives us more. James 1:5 says, "If any of you lacks wisdom, let him ask God, who gives generously to all without reproach, and it will be given him." But before we reach for the high and lofty and mysterious, we can reach for what we know. God has given us wisdom in his Word. Sometimes, our requests for wisdom are veiled appeals for loopholes. Wisdom may be more than obedience to what you already know, but it cannot be less.

Wisdom in Action

It's easy for me to forget my own foolishness. That is, until I immerse myself in the Bible's teaching on what it is to be wise. Then I can come to no other conclusion. If humility is required to even start in wisdom's direction, we ought to focus our attention there. But we do not approach humility by looking at ourselves first, but by looking at Christ.

I have a small lamp by a window in my room. Sometimes, in the morning after the sun has already risen but my room is still dark, I'll turn on the lamp just before raising the shades, and I'll watch its light disappear as sunlight floods the room. This is the way to humility. We do not try to convince ourselves that our light is dim; we put our light next to Christ's and watch ours disappear.

James contrasts wisdom from heaven with that of the world. The conflict-prone, self-interested, and inherently competitive tenor of the world's wisdom breeds disorder. It does not reward those who admit weakness; it tramples them. Instead, wisdom from above is uncorrupted by ego, peace-loving, gentle, willing to yield and show deference to others, full of mercy and good fruits, unprejudiced, without pretense, and meek (James 3:13-17). Wisdom grieves conflict while pressing toward peace; it wants the glory, honor, and fulfillment for others that fools want only for themselves. Where does James get his list for wisdom from above? From the true Wisdom, the One who *came* from above.

Often when we ask God for wisdom, we really seek guidance or direction. We have two job offers, we're getting serious with the person we've been seeing, we're trying to choose between two good options. These requests are not wrong. But to ask for wisdom from above is something different. It is to ask how to live out of the resurrection, to live like we've been resourced with every grace for godliness, and to live like we have made ourselves at home in his courts and the riches of his wisdom are always at our disposal.

I wonder, then, if we might not be better served by conceiving of wisdom as simply this: an unhurried, nontransactional courtship with Christ unfolding at his table.

From the peak of Mount Zion, the city of the living God, in a throne room filled with innumerable angels in festal gathering, Christ, the darling of creation, tends to his guests and readies for more. His is a feast without beginning or end. Fanning out like a search party, his messengers call out on his behalf, "Whoever is simple, let him turn in here!" It is staggering that One superior to angels would stoop to invite the simple-minded to his table.

By Christ and for Christ all things in heaven and on earth, visible and invisible were made (Colossians 1:16). By the breath of his mouth, he composed the soaring melodies to which Wisdom danced. From their birth, the heights and depths have ever sung his praise. As a man, Christ grew in wisdom and stature (Luke 2:52) and confounded both the wise and foolish with his incisive yet veiled wit, for it was his glory to conceal things (Proverbs 25:2). He revealed his secrets, but only over shared food and drink. The longer you'd linger, the more he'd divulge. He, the radiance of God's glory who dwells in primordial light, emits a brilliance by which all other brilliance is measured and derived. All lesser light bows in humble reverence to him. And his light overcomes every semblance of darkness and death itself.

At his table, our knowledge of Christ grows. His life and ministry instruct us. His embrace of the outcast and mercy for enemies increase our understanding of righteousness. He disciplines us for our good that we may share in that holiness we find irresistibly beautiful. We adopt his habits by proximity and as we behold his glory we are transformed, from one degree of glory to another, into the same image (2 Corinthians 3:18). He is the kind of companion who changes us.

LITURGY FOR WISDOM

*"Whoever is simple, let him turn in here!" To him
who lacks sense she says, "Come, eat of my bread and
drink of the wine I have mixed. Leave your simple
ways, and live, and walk in the way of insight."*

PROVERBS 9:4-6

Most Majestic Paragon of Wisdom, you are too kind to make
one such as me like one such as you.

I confess I falter in my attempts at wisdom, at times out of
ignorance and other times willfully so, for the way of wisdom
does not always align with my desires. You have invited me in
yet I have diverted my gaze and followed my eyes. My spirit
lags behind my flesh, my faith behind my sight.

Because my flesh longs for ease and quantifiable success, I
am enticed by the way of the simpleton. Because my desire
to be found worthy settles on the cheap and temporal, I am
seduced by the praise of man.

**"But I, through the abundance of your steadfast love, will
enter your house. I will bow down toward your holy temple
in the fear of you."**

Because I think I know best or cannot suffer the sting of being
proven wrong, I heed not correction and spurn all forms
of discipline. Because my mouth waters at the thought of
maintaining the upper hand and I glory in being right rather
than righteous, I am turned off rather than transformed by
the blows of rebuke.

"But I, through the abundance of your steadfast love, will enter your house. I will bow down toward your holy temple in the fear of you."

Because I value being entertained over being refined, I am drawn to company equipped with faulty compasses but endless diversions. Because I am the greatest and not the least in my own eyes, I am awash in selfish impulses to put myself above my neighbor.

"But I, through the abundance of your steadfast love, will enter your house. I will bow down toward your holy temple in the fear of you."

Because I believe my wisdom and not yours is supreme, I am sure of myself rather than sure of you. Because I neglect the discipline of remembrance, it is hard to imitate your fast-fading example.

"But I, through the abundance of your steadfast love, will enter your house. I will bow down toward your holy temple in the fear of you."

Wisdom Incarnate, turn my feet and affections toward you. In my own strength my heart is dull, my ears can't hear, my eyes don't see, my mind doesn't understand, and my heart treasures trash. But through the abundance of your steadfast love, I will enter your house, I will bow in fear of you alone. Through it, I will fix my gaze on you and walk in the way of insight. Yes, because of your love and your love alone will I feast at the table of the simple made wise.

Amen.

Chapter 7

RUIN REVERSED

To the Hopeless

On this mountain the Lord Almighty will prepare
a feast of rich food for all peoples,
a banquet of aged wine—
the best of meats and the finest of wines.

ISAIAH 25:6

*"I will feast the soul of the priests with abundance, and my
people shall be satisfied with my goodness," declares the LORD.*

JEREMIAH 31:14

Mingling with the clouds, Mount Zion stretched heavenward and stirred with life. You could hear the pitter patter of children's feet at play, the clangor of tambourines and plucked melodies of the lyre, the absent birdsong returned. The percussive gait of dancing merrymakers reverberated down deep in your bones while sumptuous fare and sweet wine strained the legs of every table in every home. Justice blanketed the land. It was the envy of every hill, plain, and valley.

The mountain had long forgotten the feel of festival: the sounds reverberating in its ears, the layered scents tickling its nose, life coursing through its veins, and the rhythm of revelers forming fresh footpaths on its skin. Generations had passed since the devout crowded Zion's streets, carrying sacrifices and food for the annual feasts. Even longer since the repentant had.

As the exile neared its end, comfort came to the dispersed through God's ministers. "Your warfare has ended," they were assured (Isaiah 40:2). In droves, God gathered the beleaguered back to their ancestral home. "Come, buy wine and milk without money and without price," an invitation rang (Isaiah 55:1). God beckoned his people to draw near to listen and to incline their ear so they would be satisfied, eat rich food, and, ultimately, live.

All creatures and creation partook of this homecoming feast where Yahweh was host. Food fit for nobility graced every table, and every table was garnished with things bespeaking peace. Choice meats full of marrow, aged wine, and the once taboo, sacred portion of sacrifices topped the tables. Creation, too, brought its own vibrancy to the festivities. The desert rejoiced and blossomed like the crocus—an early bloom signaling winter's end. Mountains and hills broke into song, and all trees of the field clapped their hands.

GREAT DARKNESS OF EXILE

Unlike Israel's holy days, or the feast-like experiences of the poets of Psalms and Proverbs, feasting in the prophetic books looks ahead and is most often associated with Israel's eventual restoration after exile. The prophets warned of exile should God's people persist in their disobedience. Jerusalem would be besieged, the temple destroyed, and the inhabitants of the land scattered among the land of their enemies. Should Israel repent, they could avoid destruction. Instead, they barreled forward, profaning the Sabbath, worshiping idols, perverting justice, trusting in their prosperity (or in Egypt's when theirs ran out), and mistaking the trappings of religion for devotion to God. As promised, judgment came and soon they were sore for renewal.

Exile was a time of great darkness in Israel's history. A sense of abandonment and miscarried expectation lodged itself deeply in the heart of God's people. God had promised Abraham land, descendants, a king, and laws. Above all, he'd promised Israel would be his people and he, their God. After losing a generation in the desert to disobedience after the exodus, they, at long last, inhabited the land. But now they were ejected from their land and scattered wide. Their king was deposed, and they lived under foreign rule. Laws were ignored, suppressed, or forgotten. God even gave them a new name, *Lo-ammi,* Hebrew for "not my people" (Hosea 1:9).

The land itself was denuded of all traces of life, from the fruit of the womb to the fruit of the field. Studies of famine have shown it to not only have severe physical effects, but deeply corrosive social ones as well. Thomas Keneally wrote of the 1998 Sudanese famine,

> If a village family was in extreme danger of starvation, its menfolk were permitted to spear the cow of a wealthy neighbor. This was not viewed as "charity" but as a customary transaction. But in the food crisis of 1998, landowners in southern Sudan began to fence in their cattle and prevent access to them. Fear, and the volatility of the region...produced in chiefs and village worthies a desire to close in on themselves, to protect a family's resources and to ignore needs beyond that.[1]

Israel also had a system in place that would allow those in need to share in the harvest and resources of those better off. As we saw with the Feast of Weeks in Leviticus 23, the gleaning rule prohibited God's people from reaping right up to the edge of their field and stripping their vineyard bare. Instead, they were supposed to leave the edges and the fallen grapes for the poor and sojourner (Leviticus 19; 23). But while suffering from famine, not only were standard acts of charity suspended, there was a conscious tightening of the purse toward outsiders. In Lamentations 4:4, concerns for self-preservation were such that "children beg for food, but no one gives to them."

Famished parents were forced to eat the flesh of their sons and daughters in secret (Deuteronomy 28:53-57) and death sneaked through windows to bereave families of their young (Jeremiah 9:21). Malnourished babies and children fainted of hunger on city streets (Lamentations 2:11, 19). But at the restoration this ghastly sight gives way to one where those same streets are filled with boys and girls at play (Zechariah 8:5)—a sight all the more poignant because the covenant promise to Abraham began with a child. After the exile's end, longevity would return. The image of the old lying in the dust of the street and perishing while scavenging for food (Lamentations 1:19) would give way to one of the elderly congregating along busy streets with staff in hand because of their advanced age (Zechariah 8:4).

At their misery's peak, Israel preferred death by sword to starvation (Lamentations 4:9). They were crushed when their hallowed land failed to bear fruit, when they planted much yet harvested little, when locusts consumed their fields (Deuteronomy 28:38-39), and when seeds shriveled beneath the earth while grain withered away (Joel 1:17).

They were distraught when their food supply got cut off, their storehouses lay in ruin, and their granaries sat derelict. Gone were the days of excess or of even enough. Instead, they faced unsatisfying rations of bread and vanishing cattle (Leviticus 26:26; Jeremiah 9:10). Scarcity reigned. None could foresee the array of choice meats (Isaiah 25:6), the fat portion of sacrifices (Jeremiah 31:14), and the guarantee of satisfaction awaiting them on the other side of this horror.

Before being expelled from their homes, they'd publicly decried the shortage of wine, and the vine itself mourned its loss (Isaiah 24:11).

They planted vineyards, but neither drank their wine nor gathered their grapes, because the worm got to them first (Deuteronomy 28:39).

Finally, when it came to jubilation, rather than song and dance and gladness, the merry-hearted sighed. The mirth of the tambourine and lyre were stilled, all feasting and dancing turned to mourning and songs of praise to lament, and joylessness spread as a contagion throughout the land. Neither gladness nor the voice of bride or bridegroom could be heard. All joy had reached its eventide (Isaiah 24:11 NRSV).

PRIMED FOR RETURN

While Israel awaited the end of their captivity in Babylon and wondered what it'd be like to dwell in their own land again, to rebuild and start over, God began speaking to the mountains. He gave them their new orders. Ezekiel prophesied to the mountains—even the mountains must "hear the words of the Lord" and obey, as with the words spoken to Israel. In Ezekiel 36:8-9, the prophet says, "But you, O mountains of Israel, shall shoot forth your branches and yield your fruit to my people Israel, for they will soon come home. For behold, I am for you, and I will turn to you, and you shall be tilled and sown." Mountains that had once been objects of scorn to the surrounding nations (Ezekiel 36:3) would once again drip sweet wine (Joel 3:18). And once again, rain in its season would revive them. The land that would sustain Israel was primed for their return.

To the despondent and benumbed victims of Assyria and Babylon came the prophetic picture of restoration. The prophet Isaiah described a feast of wine and choice meat. He also assured Israel that God would wipe away tears from all their faces and remove the reproach of his people (Isaiah 25:8). Right before Jeremiah tells Israel of their privileged access to the sacred portion of the sacrifice, he says God will "turn their mourning into joy...and give them gladness for sorrow" (Jeremiah 31:13).

The table captured the essence of restoration. It acted as a foil for everything dreadful, mirroring the spiritual truths of restoration on a physical level. Wine, grain, and oil, and all they represented would once more abound. Comfort and meat, fat and joy were all seen as part of the same redemptive act.

This act of deliverance so eclipsed the exodus that God boasted that rather than being known as the Lord "who brought the people of Israel up out of the land of Egypt," he would instead be known as the one "who led the offspring of the house of Israel out of the north country and out of all the countries where he had driven them" to dwell once again in their own land (Jeremiah 23:7-8). God's redemptive tour de force had been delivering the Israelites from Egypt, parting the sea for their escape, and leading them by pillar of fire and cloud through the desert. But the restoration of the exiles, the reuniting and resettling of his people in their land, would surpass it in grandeur and significance.

Against the grisly backdrop of exile, the image that emerged of restoration was a blissful reversal of ruin. Where death and hopelessness reigned in Israel's collapse, life and hope abounded at their return. Each aspect of the feast—from the food to the people to the earth that sustained them—represented a pronounced and welcome departure from the past. Yet through it all, their God remained the same.

RICH FOOD, WELL-AGED WINE, CHOICE MEAT, AND FAT FROM THE ALTAR

The feasts described in Isaiah 25 and Jeremiah 31 consist of well-aged wine, choice meat, and the fat portions of the temple sacrifices we were introduced to in chapter six. Wine held a special place in the Ancient Near Eastern imagination. At that point in its history, it was considered more a gift of the gods than a product of human ingenuity. In Jewish custom, a feast without wine would have been cause for lament and would have signaled a solemn occasion. It would have been considered a punishment or sign of calamity.[2] Wine was essential for a feast.

But well-aged wine required an extended period of peace and stability. Wine was scarce during times of conflict because vineyards were often neglected or targeted for destruction. In contrast, Zion's vineyards were not just producing grapes, but grapes for good wine. That wine was left to sit undisturbed over time to allow its lees, the dead yeast cells produced during fermentation, to settle thoroughly.[3] As they did, the resulting wine took on a much more complex flavor. To have large quantities of such high-quality wine available signaled peace, stability, and prosperity.

Returnees also feasted on rich food and meat full of marrow. What is translated as "rich food" literally means fat things. Even in peacetime, domesticated animals such as sheep and cattle were raised primarily for their wool or milk, not for slaughter, so meat was eaten relatively infrequently. In hard times, it all but disappeared from their tables. At this feast in Isaiah 25, we not only have meat fit for kings consumed by the masses, but meat full of marrow was nutrient dense and would strengthen their bodies as well. The significance of that would not be lost on a community that remembered—either through direct experience or social memory—the desperate search for nutritious food during famine.

In addition to containing valuable nutrients, fat is a well-known flavor enhancer and energy source. Inherent within it is a promise of future vitality. As flavor enhancers, fats impact the way food smells and tastes, helping release fragrance into the air when heated and distributing flavor to all it touches.

Jeremiah's poetic vision of restoration in chapter 31 features the merciful promise of homecoming and renewal where priests are again fed fat: "I will feast the soul of the priests with fatness" (verse 14). The Hebrew word for this kind of fat, *deshen*, literally referred to the ashes produced from the ritual burning of raw animal fat on the altar for offerings. The raw fat, also known as suet (or, in Hebrew, *heleb*), was burned and rose as a pleasing fragrance to the Lord (Leviticus 1:9), just as Christ also served as a fragrant offering and sacrifice to God (Ephesians 5:2). The Hebrew word for this kind of fat became synonymous with abundance and surplus.

In the time of temple sacrifices, however, priests were forbidden from partaking of the fat. Leviticus 3:16 states, "All the fat belongs to the Lord." Yet here in Jeremiah, just verses before the new covenant, which the blood of Christ fulfills, is given, our Lord offers the sacrificed fat as the crown dish to the restored members of his royal priesthood. This priestly designation goes as far back as the giving of the Law at Mount Sinai and is reiterated in Isaiah's address to a people in limbo when he promises they will one day eat the wealth of the nations (Isaiah 61:6). It is a designation that extends to us (1 Peter 2:9). Those priests' souls were promised the prime portion in the fat of the altar. Likewise, God promises us the prime portion in Christ, so that we, like them, may be satisfied with his goodness. The most precious and sacred has been offered to us. If he has given us that, will he not also graciously give us all things?

BETWEEN TWO PICTURES

In the wake of natural disasters like floods or hurricanes, aerial images are released of the destruction for comparison to show the scale of the damage. Some media sources have begun to superimpose the before and after images over each other in such a way that the *before* image is only revealed by moving a vertical slider over the *after* image. With the prophetic images of restoration, we roll the slider over the image of Assyrian and Babylonian destruction to reveal not the before image, but an after one that even exceeds the pre-invasion days in glory. Zechariah 9:12 says God will restore to them double for their hardship.

Christians today live somewhere between these two pictures with the realities of each bearing down on our lives, bringing both sorrow and exceeding joy. We live in a time where we've begun to see and experience the latter glory, but don't yet see it in full. We long for the day when the picture of renewal is complete.

Was Israel like disaster survivors today? Their lives are upended only to anticipate heartbreaking, unrecognizable ruin when finally able to journey home. What will be left of what was once so dear? Will their home be intact? Would the road back even be navigable? But over and again, the prophets painted a different picture of return. Jeremiah assured them that on their return "they will be radiant over the goodness of the LORD" (31:12) and that with tears of repentance they will sing aloud on the heights of Zion with laughter and joy.

Living Within the Feast

Sometimes we find ourselves sitting in darkness, with the broken fragments of future hopes strewn at the heads of every street, carrying in our souls the disappointment of lives that turned out bitterly different than we'd planned. We fall prey to the lie that resources are scarce and we live in a time of famine, although our God never comes up short. We work hard to convince ourselves that day will not break, while hope wilts in the dark. Return can seem unthinkable.

What recourse do we have when streams of sorrow overtake us? When the decay before our eyes wearies us and the world's brokenness infiltrates our hearts? When we are homesick for a goodness and abundance that feel impossibly out of reach?

We live within the feast. We take a seat at the table of hope. We remember that our desperate search for nourishment has come to an end. The meat, the wine, and the fat before us tell us how we ought to live. How we can live. How we were made to live. They remind us who we are and who we worship. They point us to the reality of a sure and splendid reversal of ruin. They situate us within the correct story, a story that arcs toward redemption and renewal, not abandonment. The meal reaffirms the promises and identities we can cling to when the pall of death—in all its guises—leaves us paralyzed beneath its shadow. We are guests of the King, members of the royal family. We make ourselves at home before a table that speaks of peace, stability, and death-defying deliverance. We bask in the presence of the one who catches our tears and who alone can transform them into praise. We live in famine no more.

Since famine has ended, we live generously. While the exile made generosity untenable, restoration revived it. It lifted the embargo on sharing with those in need. Generosity had languished in the land during the worst of the Assyrian and Babylonian aggressions, but nothing about the restoration could keep it from flourishing.

The feast of restoration teaches us we are a peculiar people. We are a people whose source for all things begins in God, who no longer fear famine, who are being rebuilt and made new. We are a people whose warfare has ended and who have been made secure by God alone. The goodness of our God satisfies us. His extravagant mercy and grace strike us dumb. Indeed, we are people of hope.

Ezekiel continues the theme of reversal to say the desolate cities will be inhabited and the waste places rebuilt. Both man and beast will multiply and once again bear fruit.

> I will cause you to be inhabited as in your former times, and will do more good to you than ever before. Then you will know that I am the Lord. I will let people walk on you, even my people Israel. And they shall possess you, and you shall be their inheritance, and you shall no longer bereave them of children (36:11-12).

The land that was to sustain them did so at the direction of the Creator. We also are a people being rebuilt and renewed. Living between

Christ's first and second coming, we occupy the period of redemptive history where restoration is both a reality secured for us in Christ that we get to enjoy now, and one being actively worked out in our lives day by day. It is also true that we are still, as Peter noted, considered exiles today (1 Peter 2:11). So we straddle having been made new yet still being under construction, being restored but not completely untouched by the ills of exile.

Though God allowed Israel to be afflicted, he would use it for their good, to refine them. And as we feast on all we have in Christ, we, too, are being transformed into the glorious creatures God originally intended. Exile was but an instrument in the refiner's hand—rather than exilic judgment leading to our death, trial disciplines us unto life and glory.

As we learned above, where there is warfare, there is no wine. At least, not of the caliber or in the quantity present at the restoration feast. The wine reminds us what time it is and at whose table we recline. The God who rouses the mountains into fruitfulness and expels Israel's enemies from his people's land offers us abundant peace.

In our limbo between exile and restoration, we are certain to have enemies, but this does not preclude us from also having peace. In the restoration song of Isaiah 26, Israel will sing—on that same day on that same mountain at that same feast—that God keeps in perfect peace all whose minds are stayed on him. They will sing with confidence, "O LORD, you will ordain peace for us, for you have indeed done for us all our works" (verse 12). We can revel in our peace when we seek it in him. Holding tight to his promises, we can see through our enemies to their eventual and utter defeat. We can see the peace he secures for us.

PEOPLE OF HOPE

Therefore, we are people of hope. Scripture never makes the false promise that life will be easy. On the contrary, we're told we will encounter trouble as a matter of course: "In this life you will have trouble" (John 16:33). Even more so if we desire to live godly lives: "Indeed, all who desire to live a godly life in Christ Jesus will be persecuted" (2 Timothy 3:12). But is there anything we can do besides hunker down in the darkness and ride it out till the end? How does the feast help us escape our despair?

First, we look before and behind. The restoration is not just nearer to us than it was Israel, but the Restorer has come. He does not dwell with us on the mountain; he dwells within us and has brought his feast there. Spiritual myopia suffocates hope. Shortsightedness barricades our escape. Focusing only on the present hardship while either ignoring God's past faithfulness or failing to look forward to the completion of God's work of renewal makes despair like quicksand. Instead, we open our heart to God's story in Scripture, in our lives, and in the testimony of fellow witnesses of his grace around us. Regardless of how far back ruin and devastation reach in our stories—even if it feels like we are enmeshed in them now—we have hope. And we live out of that hope not by wishful thinking, but through God's Spirit and the routine rehearsal of the truth that his faithfulness will continue in the future as it has in the past. From the bowels of agony, one of the afflicted turns the corner from despair to hope in Lamentations 3:21-23: "This I call to mind, and therefore I have hope: The steadfast love of the LORD never ceases; his mercies never come to an end; they are new every morning; great is your faithfulness."

Further, to be people of hope, we cling to God and his promises. Again, in the song Israel will sing recounting the story of their return to their land as they head to feast, they recount, "O LORD, in distress they sought you; they poured out a whispered prayer when your discipline was upon them" (Isaiah 26:16). The Hebrew reads more emphatically, unconventionally placing the object of the sentence first, "God they sought in their distress," suggesting it was God and God alone they sought. And, even though all they could do was whisper a prayer under the weight of his discipline, they called out all the same.

Finally, we trust he is working. God comforted those in exile: "Say to those who have an anxious heart, 'Be strong; fear not! Behold, your God will come with vengeance, with the recompense of God. He will come and save you'" (Isaiah 35:3-4). That was true for Israel, and in Christ it's true for us. When Israel returned, Isaiah says they would return with the cheer, "This is our God, we trusted in him, and he saved us. This is the LORD, we trusted in him" (25:9). What joy finds those who can say they always knew he could do it, who believe against all odds that he who began his good work in us is faithful to complete it.

If we're not vigilant, rather than being the "prisoners of hope" (Zechariah 9:12) we are called and compelled to be, we can easily become prisoners of despair. The faithful in exile knew this tendency toward self-pity well when one lamented, "Look and see if there is any sorrow like my sorrow" (Lamentations 1:12). Alongside Jeremiah's description of the restoration feast, he delivers this guarantee from God, "I will satisfy the weary soul, and every languishing soul I will replenish" (31:25). And again in Isaiah, "He will swallow up death forever, the Sovereign LORD will wipe away the tears from all faces; he will remove his people's disgrace from all earth" (25:8 NIV). Ahead we see replenishment and satisfaction, and behind we see its purchase. We cling to his promises. We put our trust in him. From the ends of the earth, songs of praise and glory to the Righteous One were heard from the lips of the returned. We look forward to singing as they sang, "Behold, this is our God; we have waited for him" (Isaiah 25:9).

FROM ONE DEGREE OF GLORY TO THE NEXT

I can only imagine what it was like for Israel to return to their land with their last memories being those of utter destruction. They were faced with the task of trying to overwrite the painful memories—whether experienced or inherited—of the devastation, the hopelessness, of resigned desperation. To these, God spoke those oft-quoted words of Jeremiah about God's plans for our hope and future. "'For I know the plans I have for you,' declares the LORD, 'plans to prosper you and not to harm you, plans to give you hope and a future'" (Jeremiah 29:11 NIV). How their souls must have leapt at the promised triumph of joy and plenty over every inch of the land!

Isaiah warned that far more pain would come before healing. At the same time, he also encouraged them that not only would they get a new name at the restoration, but so would their beloved land: A City Not Forsaken.

A few years after college, I had the chance to visit a Japanese friend from Hiroshima in her hometown. We made our way to the Peace Memorial Park, the site where the atomic bomb first dropped in 1945. With the exception of the A-Bomb Dome, one of the only structures to partially survive the blast, the previous devastation was undetectable to the naked eye. What I saw, standing there at ground zero in front of the arched cenotaph with my friend, was a vibrant, bustling city restored. No site in history had known greater devastation, but looking around, no one would've known had they not been told.

One day this will be true of us as well. Every day, God's Spirit nudges the slider further in the direction of an ever more complete renewal. As heirs of God's promises and celebrants at his feast, we trust in him alone and feast as we and our circumstances are transformed. And as we lift to parched lips fine wine from ground once barren, the Spirit molds us anew into his image, from one degree of glory to the next.

LITURGY FOR RESTORATION

God Who Gathers, no one finds us like you do nor has your reach:

From the heights of heaven you make us out amidst black chasms of hopelessness and despair and mercifully arrange for our rescue. We are unworthy beneficiaries of your far-sighted covenant love.

Forgive us for giving oxygen to the lie that because we cannot see you, you are absent; for letting circumstances convince us you are the God Who Forsakes, not the God Who Pursues.

When the maelstroms of life spit us out, disoriented and distraught, on foreign land may we be anchored by the conviction that you will gather us back, for this is your glorious boast.

Sustain us, that we may access the table you have prepared for us in your presence where there is fullness of joy.

God Who Rebuilds, there is no destruction you cannot undo:

Since creation you have brought forth beauty out of nothing. Your heart aches for all vestige of brokenness, for wholeness and integrity were your design.

We are quick to focus on the shards of shattered dreams rather than on the hands that can puzzle those pieces back together. We cannot see past our crumbling surroundings to your tested faithfulness. Have mercy on us, O God.

May we not hastily rebuild on our own nor seek to dodge the trying but necessary fires you use to skim away the dross.

Rebuild us, Master Architect, that our latter glory might bring you renown.

God Who Restores, you bring life from death, even death long settled:

You seek the weary and weathered to renew their strength. You confuse the aims of calamity, using it to draw us to you, our true source of life.

In the face of scarcity and decline we falter under the weight you died to carry for us. We have little appetite for the spiritual nourishment our souls require and which you alone provide. We turn now to you.

Dress our wounds when we hemorrhage hope. Free us from worldly attachments that compete for our affection. May the joy of the redeemed return.

Restore us, Faithful Lord, that we may sing once more from the heights of Zion.

O God who brings back your people:

Gather us to yourself, rebuild what is broken, restore what has been lost. Though you have humbled us, you will exalt us again. We seek your grace that we may eat and drink to the full of the feast you set before us.

Through the kindness of Christ who alone satisfies we come.

Amen.

Chapter 8

A FEAST FOR UNDERSTANDING

To Those in Need of Repair

Then he said to them, "Go your way. Eat the fat and drink sweet wine and send portions to anyone who has nothing ready, for this day is holy to our Lord. And do not be grieved, for the joy of the LORD is your strength."...And all the people went their way to eat and drink and to send portions and to make great rejoicing, because they had understood the words that were declared to them.

NEHEMIAH 8:10,12

The prophets spoke of a day when the remnant would return to their land. The books of Ezra and Nehemiah, along with Haggai, Zechariah, and Malachi, show what happens after they do. These books, unlike most we've seen so far, are not well known. On the surface, the episode in the life of Israel captured in Nehemiah 8:1-8 may lack the flare, gravitas, or urgency that drove the feasts of the poets and prophets and the observation of special days. But, even in this wallflower of a feast, tucked away in the last book of the Hebrew Bible, we see God wooing his own back to himself.

Construction projects dominate Ezra and Nehemiah, two historical books that, until the Middle Ages, appeared as one in the Hebrew canon.[1] Since strategic and visionary oversight of complex building projects fills their pages, people most often reference them when teaching about leadership or launching church capital campaigns. But Nehemiah is about more than just construction and godly leadership. It's not primarily about the temple, nor is it primarily about the wall. It's about God's Law in the life of God's people, a people on the cusp of hope.

As exile trudged on, it left in its wake depleted land, communities, spirits, and bodies. But the anticipation of return refused to recede within their minds while they lived in foreign land under foreign rule and longed for the grandeur and greatness they'd lost. The land, as we saw in earlier chapters, was invaluable to the people of God. Finally, it had been returned. Renewal and revival lie ahead...right?

Rebuilding the Temple

At Persian king Cyrus' decree, Zerubbabel led the first wave of exiles out of captivity back to Jerusalem in 538 BC to rebuild the temple (Ezra 1:2). The Lord commanded Zerubbabel to rebuild and stirred up his spirit to work (Haggai 1). At least 42,000 people—servants and singers not included—returned. Zechariah assured Zerubbabel that God would do the work, "Not by might, nor by power, but by the Spirit, says the LORD of hosts" (Zechariah 4:6). First, the returned exiles rebuilt the temple altar so they could resume offerings there (Ezra 3:3). A year later, they began laying the temple's foundation. After setting the last dressed stone in place, the returnees gathered to celebrate. Some were overcome with bitter tears because the new temple's foundation did not match the former's in glory (Ezra 3:10-13). To them, Zechariah said, "Do not despise these small beginnings, for the LORD rejoices to see the work begin" (Zechariah 4:10 NLT). Others shouted for joy. Weeping and jubilee, equal in volume and vigor, drifted into the distance, carrying the mixed feelings of the community to the outskirts of the city.

With the tailwind of the two successes of the rebuilt temple altar and foundation propelling them, the people continued to work on the temple itself. Despite strong opposition from Samaritans who occupied the land, construction on the rest of the temple continued, and eventually, it was rebuilt in 515 BC (Ezra 6:13-18). God's people had regained a central fixture of their identity and worship.

The temple was of immense importance to the people of Israel. God himself dwelled there, and it housed the ark of the covenant. After King Solomon built the temple, he dedicated it, marveling, "But will God indeed dwell on the earth? Behold, heaven and the highest heaven cannot contain you; how much less this house that I have built!" (1 Kings 8:27). From then on, no ground was more sacred. It was also the site of the three pilgrimage feasts. Religious life centered around it. And even in exile, the diaspora regularly prayed in the direction the temple once stood (Daniel 6:10; 1 Kings 8:29), each time rekindling their hope for a future return.[2] The temple stabilized a scattered nation.

But a dark side to their temple veneration infiltrated the national psyche as well. Jeremiah 7:4 suggests the temple had become a source of false confidence; its existence allowed Israel to continue living contrary to God's Law with imagined impunity. Jeremiah cautioned a people living opposed to God's Law, "Do not trust in these deceptive words: 'This is the temple of the LORD, the temple of the LORD, the temple of the LORD.'" The temple's mere existence led to the presumption of safety. Surely, God would not allow his dwelling place to be attacked. Surely, he would defend his own house.

But God never meant for the temple to replace obedience. Affiliation with a house of worship did not a worshiper make. The faithfulness of the people was not fixed to the temple, or even to the sacrifices offered there. But rather, to their wholehearted adherence to the Law of the Lord. God did not despise the temple, but he would not accept as a substitute the charade of worship when he was after their hearts. Before exile, the temple building itself had lulled them into a false sense of immunity, and their unrepentant lives of injustice and syncretism proved it.

Sixty years later, King Artaxerxes, in keeping with the Persian policy of religious tolerance, sent Ezra, scribe and priest, back to Jerusalem with a letter. It freed any Jew who so wished to return with him to their homeland. So Ezra returned to lead a series of religious reforms with the second wave of exiled Jews. He was on a mission: "Ezra had set his heart to study the Law of the Lord, and to do it and to teach his statutes and rules in Israel" (Ezra 7:10). King Artaxerxes also sent him with the ancient equivalent of a blank check: silver, gold, and money enough to do whatever seemed good to him and his brothers to do (Ezra 7:18). He had unrestricted access to the king's treasury.

As he set out, Ezra acknowledged the Lord's hand behind the king's favor, "Blessed be the Lord, the God of our fathers, who put such a thing as this into the heart of the king, to beautify the house of the Lord that is in Jerusalem" (Ezra 7:27). The book of Ezra ends with its namesake doing the Lord's work among the Lord's people, reprimanding them for sin that had crept into the community and leading them in confession (Ezra 9–10).

Repairing the Wall

The story of the exiles' return continues in the book of Nehemiah, which opens with news reaching Nehemiah of the state of his people and the city wall. "The remnant there in the province who had survived the exile is in great trouble and shame. The wall of Jerusalem is broken down, and its gates are destroyed by fire" (Nehemiah 1:3). Survivors of exile suffer disgrace; the wall sits in shambles. Overwhelmed with grief at the condition of his beloved people and land, he petitions God for the favor of King Artaxerxes to grant him leave to go back to Jerusalem to help.

Nehemiah is governor and cupbearer to the king, and one day he appears, long faced, before him. The king takes notice, "Why are you sad, seeing you are not sick?" (Nehemiah 2:2). How could he be happy knowing the land of his ancestors lay in ruin? He sought permission to return to repair the broken-down city wall. Nehemiah is one of those books, like Lamentations, where God is only spoken of but doesn't speak. Yet these books clearly acknowledge he is active behind the scenes. The king agrees and, like Ezra, Nehemiah credits this to the Lord: "The king granted me what I asked, for the good hand of my God was upon me" (Nehemiah 2:8). Nehemiah is given letters to present to other governors he may encounter along the way to let him pass through their land unbothered and is also given a letter to the keeper of the king's forest for timber to use in rebuilding. He will go tend to the people and the wall.

Nehemiah encounters difficulty and opposition from influential people as construction gets underway. While the opposition mock and threaten him, the people build with weapons in one hand and tools in the other. Construction moved forward, and in 52 days the city wall was repaired. It was a community effort; whole households joined together in the work.

City walls were important not only to residents of Jerusalem but to most of antiquity. Those hoping to occupy themselves with more than the defense of their safety wanted fortified walls. No one felt safe in a defenseless city. David Frye, in his history of city walls, writes, "No invention in human history played a greater role in creating and shaping civilization."[3] City walls didn't just create a sense of safety, but freed residents to develop other pursuits and diversions. Frye continues,

The birth of walls set human societies on divergent paths, one leading to self-indulgent poetry, the other to taciturn militarism. But the first path also pointed to much more—science, mathematics, theater, art—while the other brought its followers only to a dead end, where a man was nothing except a warrior and all labor devolved upon the women.[4]

A rebuilt wall promised changes for civic life. The psyche of walled cities changed: they went from being places where every man was a soldier to being a place where a diversity of occupations could flourish, and life could move beyond survival. "Everywhere farmers settled, they fortified their villages...Entire communities pitched in to make their villages secure."[5] Walls let people live and gave them a sense of peace and security.

However, God through Moses had warned that like the temple, the city wall could become a snare. In Deuteronomy 28:52, Moses lays out curses for covenant disobedience: "They will lay siege to all the cities throughout your land until the high fortified walls *in which you trust* fall down" (emphasis mine). They, like we, were constantly seeking security, but never quite in the right place. Neither the temple nor city walls were the center of their identity or security as people of God.

REPAIRING THE PEOPLE

With the temple rebuilt and wall repaired, focus shifts inward in Nehemiah 8 to rebuilding a broken-down people. Ezra reappears. But this time, it's not at the king's orders, nor even of his own volition. At the request of the people, he re-enters the story. On the eve of a renewed commitment to God's covenant and Law (Nehemiah 9–10), the people feast.

The first day of the seventh month, all Israel gathered as one and ordered Ezra to bring out the Law. To gather at the temple would have restricted participation to men only, so they assembled at the Water Gate instead. All were present: men, women, and children—any who could understand. Ezra stood before all the people on a platform, flanked by 13 other experts in the Law. He began by blessing the Lord to "Amens" and lifted hands from all the people, and all the people bowed with faces to the ground to worship. The Law was hallowed. From early morning to midday—at least five and a half hours longer than most of us would last—he read to all the people from the book. For six hours they stood, gripped by what they heard, their attention undivided (Nehemiah 8:3). As Ezra read, his podium mates went down and mixed among the crowd, explaining to them what they heard and giving the sense, so the people could understand. An analogy here, a paraphrase there, defining a word for a child. Understanding swept through the crowd. As it settled into all the peoples' bones, they wept. Sobs competed with the sound of Ezra's reading. Conviction, remorse, and lament unraveled them, and the mood turned somber. Their insides turned as they recalled where they'd gone wrong, the warnings they'd ignored, and all the needless pain and shame they'd suffered.

But grief would not rule the day. That was not the intended end of God's Law. Ezra, Nehemiah, and the Levites calmed all the people,

> This day is holy to the LORD your God. Do not mourn
> or weep...Go your way. Eat the fat and drink sweet wine
> and send portions to anyone who has nothing ready, for
> this day is holy to our Lord. And do not be grieved, for
> the joy of the LORD is your strength (Nehemiah 8:9-10).

So they return to their homes rejoicing because they had understood the words spoken to them (Nehemiah 8:12). For joy and feasting were the ultimate aims of God's Law. Grief and lament were but stops along the way.

A United Grassroots Return

A spirit of unity energizes this scene in Nehemiah. "All the people" are the main characters of this section, and the phrase occurs nine times in twelve verses. They also gathered "as one man" (Nehemiah 8:1). The return to the Law was not isolated to a few, but rather, a desire for it had galvanized all. Further, the people themselves initiated the reading of the Law. It was a grassroots return, not top-down. Mervin Breneman writes of this moment in Israel's history, "It is significant that this reading of the law and the worship service were not centered in the temple and not controlled by the priesthood. From this time on in Judaism, the Torah was more important than the temple."[6]

It was also clear from the people's response that they engaged deeply with what they heard. Conviction moved them to tears. Their hunger for God's Word united and empowered them. It led them to an honest reckoning with their past that began to restore their present. They feasted first on the Word at the Water Gate, then moved the feast to their homes.

Fat and Sweet Wine

The Word they heard was rich, and they'd been encouraged to respond to it with joy. They were told to go home and eat *mashman*, yet another word rendered "fat" in English that connotes richness. This word is also used in Genesis 27:28 when Isaac blesses Jacob, later renamed Israel: "May God give you of the dew of heaven and of the fatness of the earth" (Genesis 35:10). In addition to the fat, they drank wine, sweet as the aftertaste of God's Law rightly understood.

The call to feast throughout Scripture, as we've seen, is accompanied by the call to share with those in need. This shows up in the Passover meal, in the Feast of Weeks, in communion, and also here. None should luxuriate in their abundance while others lack the basic necessities for survival. Stinginess was inconsistent with a community renewed in its understanding of the Law of God.

In his book *The Hidden Life of Trees*, Peter Wohlleben shares about the science of the inner life of trees. How their roots support each other, how they communicate with each other, and how they grow. In his chapter entitled "Social Security," he looks at how trees grow together, shedding light on evidence that debunks the idea that trees grow best spaced farther apart so they aren't competing for resources. He writes,

> The trees, it seems, are equalizing differences between the strong and the weak. Whether they are thick or thin, all members of the same species are using light to produce the same amount of sugar per leaf. This equalization is taking place underground through the roots...Whoever has an abundance of sugar hands some over; whoever is running short gets help...It's a bit like the way social security systems operate to ensure individual members of society don't fall too far behind...When trees grow together, nutrients and water can be optimally divided among them all so that each tree can grow into the best tree it can be...A tree can be only as strong as the forest that surrounds it.[7]

This is the picture of a community shaped by an understanding of God's Law. Earlier in Nehemiah 5, Nehemiah rebukes the people for exacting interest from each other and selling their own into slavery. Oppression and mistreatment of the poor had accompanied the remnant back to the land. But once they understood the words of the Law, generosity and concern for neighbors should become the new normal. It's what the covenant community does.

THE SPRINGBOARD OF UNDERSTANDING

The people feasted because they understood. Understanding that neither mobilizes us for mission nor rouses our affections is a mere retention of words. Understanding that doesn't make its way into our everyday is trivia. The message of the Bible is not rightly understood if it stops with our grief over our sin or does not change our lives. It does not end in grief but in hope. It does not leave us stuck but empowered by God's Spirit. Kidner writes,

> We are brought to the heart of the matter. The completed walls, the throng and the conviviality were all peripheral or secondary. To have understood what God was saying was what made the occasion. It was a step from blind religiousness towards some degree of divine human fellowship. Its full flowering would be in the new covenant with its assurance, "they shall all know me"; but the old covenant already held much promise of its successor.[8]

In Deuteronomy 29:4, Moses tells the people of Israel, "But to this day the LORD has not given you a heart to understand or eyes to see or ears to hear." This would come with the greater covenant promised of which we, in greater fullness than they did, enjoy.

THE JOY OF THE LORD

"The joy of the LORD is your strength" is a surprisingly well-known verse given the relative obscurity of the context out of which it arises. To stem the flow of a nation's tears, Israel's civic and religious leaders spoke these very words to them to calm the penitent remnant with feet back on soil ever so dear to them. The encouragement was all the more striking given their setting before the city wall and temple. The temple wasn't their strength, and neither was the wall. Only the joy of the Lord—impregnable, inexhaustible, invigorating, and inalienable— could be their strength. Everything else had proven bitterly it could not.

The word translated strength means "a place or means of safety, protection." It is also translated as fortress and defense, from a word meaning fortified place. The joy of the Lord was Israel's means of safety and protection. To grasp joy through the Law was as good as a city wall. A regathered people was a promise kept, but understanding was the foundation on which they would be built.[9] The people realized that their restoration could not be complete without God's Law, which he had given as part of his covenant promises to his people, along with the land they'd come to reinhabit. Grief was a by-product of their exilic death, but the joy of the Lord was a defining feature of their postexilic rebirth. Like the city walls, it would bring relief and gladness.

There is a time and place for solemnity, but this was a time for joy—so they should feast. Unlike others we've seen, this feast wasn't an invitation to remember, nor did it mark a landmark moment in Israel's history that they should later observe. It wasn't metaphorical. Their tables were spread with sweets and fatty meats. It was the celebratory overflow of the Law being consumed and understood.

A Festal Return to Themselves

Their return to glory began with infrastructure. They first began rebuilding the temple—the place where their God dwelt, an emblem of their status as the chosen and favored people of the one true God. Organized by visionary leadership, they began the work, but it was not without opposition. In addition to outside hostility, they themselves grew weary. There were times their progress stalled, yet the temple went up. The wall of the city too. And here we see that the joy of the Lord *was* their infrastructure.

The people probably thought they could breathe a big sigh of relief. Even though the temple was a far cry from its former glory, as was the wall, they were hopeful about what progress had been made and what lay ahead. The land, the temple, their city, since as long as they could remember, these things made them who they were. They distinguished them as God's people. Brick by brick, they were strengthened to rebuild their nation. The exemplary leadership of Ezra and Nehemiah gave them hope. God had sent them good leaders who would get them back on track. All signs pointed to the dawn of a new age of Jerusalem. A new beginning. A fresh start. A welcome change from the heartache and loss they knew all too well. Amidst all this, the people knew that a return to the Law must also play a part in their new life. Kidner writes, "What is strikingly apparent is the royal reception given to the Word of God. This day was to prove a turning-point. From now on, the Jews would be predominantly 'the people of a book'."[10]

Like them, our understanding of God is meant to lead to joy. Joy is the effect of understanding on the soul. For the people of God, if understanding stops with grief, it has not fully flowered. For us, as for the remnant, a true return from exile is an inward one rooted in God's Word. There can be no return without it. While the temple and the walls may have ostensibly deterred Israel's neighbors, the Lord's joy ultimately kept them safe. We have plenty of our own versions of these false protections as well: material prosperity, church attendance, gifting, pedigree, good deeds. No matter how many of these we have stocked up, none are as sure as the joy of the Lord. Only when Israel returned to his Law could their revival and renaissance begin. The Law would allow them to reclaim their identity and reacquaint themselves with God's. An attentiveness and understanding of it would fortify them more effectively than any structure their hands could build. This was God's true source of joy. Yes, he wanted a house where his spirit could dwell, and yes, he wanted peace for them on all sides from their enemies, but having those without being understood by his people was joyless for him. He got no joy out of being worshiped but not known.[11] But to be known and understood delighted him.

As for the people, the religious buildings of a set-apart people could not set them apart spiritually. Their buildings could not keep them from blending in with the surrounding nations or living as they lived. The fortified walls of a city could offer no protection. Sin and wayward desire could breach them. But an understanding of God that reached beyond guilt over sin into wells of joy at God's faithfulness would both set them apart and keep them safe. It was the lack of understanding evidenced in their lives of sin that led to exile and it would be nothing but their understanding seen through lives of obedience that would restore them. The end of the story was not grief over sin and exile, but joy in the Lord as renewal.

The book of Nehemiah closes with a revival. The people are led in a lengthy confession and renew their commitment to the covenant, even signing their name to it (Nehemiah 9–10). Next, they dedicated the city walls with great rejoicing: "They offered great sacrifices that day and rejoiced, for God had made them rejoice with great joy; and the women and children also rejoiced. And the joy of Jerusalem was heard far away" (Nehemiah 12:43). This time, that joy was unmingled with sorrow.

Nehemiah instituted his final reforms and as we read, we are hopeful that maybe this time, with exile behind them and having gained understanding, things will go smoothly for the nation of Israel. But, before long, they'd drifted again from God's ways and the book ends with the people backsliding (Nehemiah 13). And that's where the Hebrew Bible ends too. The people of God are back in his land, the temple and city walls have been rebuilt, the Law has been re-implemented in worship, the people have confessed and recommitted to God. Then sin again rears its ugly head. Old Testament scholar Gordon F. Davies writes, "Ezra and Nehemiah cannot keep the people from sinning again...But their rhetoric...has put into motion an interpretive mechanism that holds the Law before the people as a continuous vehicle for conversion."[12] Even if they failed, Israel showed a commitment to the Law unparalleled before exile.

We, too, should be people of the book. We, too, should turn to it for the repair of our souls. Corporately, we should commit to it to see the church mature and prosper. A deep reverence for God as communicated through his Law fuels our worship and obedience. And our understanding of him is our joy and strength.

What's your city wall? What is the temple in which you make your boast apart from Christ? I worked in vocational ministry briefly after college and, without even realizing it, made ministry my god. It was only after God called me out of it, wrecking my sense of identity, stability, and worth, that I realized I'd put my trust in that rather than in him. I'd looked to it to save me. Isn't it true that so often we only discover our walls after they fall?

Today I look to professional accomplishments, talents, and relationships to feel secure. But the abundant life we're promised does not grow out of this soil. It grows from the fertile ground of God's living Word rousing our hearts by the power of the Spirit. It flowers as we believe in our deepest depths its truths and rest our souls in the finished work of Christ. No building in the world can so settle us.

We very much need today what Israel needed then. The sin and fallenness of the world leave in its wake exhausted communities, spirits, and bodies. We need to be repaired and renewed. Precisely when we feel we cannot escape our brokenness or when our attempts at self-construction hit snags, can we find our renewal in the same place Israel found theirs: in a united, grassroots recovery of the Word as our strength. We can sit with it—souls laid bare—and let understanding settle into our bones, allowing the knowledge of who God is and who we are to transform conviction and sorrow into joy. Only then can we go our way, feasting.

LITURGY FOR UNDERSTANDING

O Lord God of heaven,

the great, mighty, and awesome God who keeps covenant and steadfast love,

let your ear be attentive to the prayer of your servants.

Enlighten the eyes of our heart, O Lord, and grant us, O God, understanding.

O Lord, repair your people.

Make us as one, according to your good pleasure.

We have strayed from your way, and division, like weeds, has overtaken us.

We have missed the beauty of unity; confusing an act of worship done

through you and to you,

as being through us and to us.

May we find the means and ends of our unity in you.

Though it costs us, may we find it rich and sweet.

Enlighten the eyes of our heart, O Lord, and grant us, O God, understanding.

O Lord, repair your people.

We've distorted, stretched, or ignored your Law for our gain.

Grant us a hunger for your Word, and restore in us an appetite for truth.

Captivate us by your nature revealed within its pages,
that we might linger long and find it rich and sweet.
Enlighten the eyes of our heart, O Lord, and grant us, O God,
understanding.

O Lord, we look to you for our strength.
We have misplaced our confidence and boast.
Keep us from rigging the temporalities of this world into our
security;
graciously topple our every tower of misfounded trust.
May rejoicing abound among and within us because of your
faithfulness.
Enlighten the eyes of our heart, O Lord, and grant us, O God,
understanding.

O Lord, God of heaven, we come.
In the path of your commands, repair us.
In our standing united as one, repair us
that we might not blend indistinguishably in with the world,
but be fortified and sanctified by you.

Amen.

Chapter 9

FEASTS OF MERCY

To Those Who Are Poor, Disabled, and Lacking Honor

"Go out at once into the streets and lanes of the city and bring in here those who are poor, those with disabilities, those who are blind, and those who are limping." And later the slave said, "Master, what you commanded has been done, and still there is room."

LUKE 14:21-22 NASB

The greatest profuseness in a feast appears neither delightful nor genteel, unless beautified by order. And therefore it is absurd that cooks and waiters should be solicitous what dish must be brought first, what next, what placed in the middle, and what last;...and yet that the guests should be seated promiscuously, and no respect be had to age, honor, or the like; no distinguishing order by which the man in dignity might be honored, the inferior learn to give place, and the disposer be exercised in distinguishing what is proper and convenient. For it is not rational that, when we walk or sit down to discourse, the best man should have the best place, and not the same order be observed at table; or that the entertainer should in civility drink to one before another, and yet make no difference in their seats.[1]

These words from Plutarch's *Table Talk* reflect a mindset common within the first century Greco-Roman culture in which Jesus lived. The honor and dignity of banquet guests should be visible from their seating arrangement. If honor is marked in every other sphere of life, why not also the banquet table? We see this in modern life as well with things like wedding receptions and formal dinners. In some cultures, even more common shared meals retain an emphasis on status in seating arrangement. Jesus' views, however, diverge sharply from this, as we see in the banquet parables of Luke 14.

JESUS AND THE TABLE

So far, we've feasted to remember, to mark the beginning and end of harvest season, to gain wisdom, and to celebrate understanding. We've had victory feasts, gorged ourselves on hope, and seen thirst turn to satisfaction in the wilderness. As we enter the New Testament, the feasts we encounter in the teachings of Jesus are first and foremost about God's kingdom. While they look to the future, they also hold significance for the kingdom unfolding here and now. They reveal how to enter the kingdom and what his kingdom is like. Now we feast to understand God's kingdom.

Jesus often healed, taught, and had run-ins with the religious elite of his day all at the table. The parables of the wedding feast and great banquet in Luke 14 where guests scramble for the best seats and where surprising guests were invited to a meal contain all three. The identity of the dinner guests in verses 12-24 is of special interest. Do people who are poor, those with disabilities, those who are blind, and those who are limping stand for some marginalized religious group or the Gentiles?

Or, do they themselves receive an invitation to the banquet? Juxtaposing the highest with the lowest social statuses in this parable suggests Jesus is emphasizing the inverted hierarchy of his kingdom. His was a kingdom of reversals.

KINGDOM REVERSALS

From its earliest chapters, themes reverberate throughout Luke that challenge both popular Greek and Jewish thought: divine reversals, concern for those who are poor, and the banquet motif. After learning she is pregnant, Mary extols a God of reversals who "vindicates the downtrodden and ministers to the hungry."[2] In her Magnificat, the lowly are exalted, and rulers brought low.

Jesus launches his public ministry with the message of his anointing "to preach good news to the poor, proclaim liberty to captives, recover sight for the blind, and set the oppressed free" (Luke 4:18). When John the Baptist sends his disciples to inquire if Jesus is the one they've been waiting for, Jesus points to the fruit of his ministry: "People who were blind receive sight, people who limped walk, people with leprosy are cleansed and people who were deaf hear, dead people are raised up, and people who are poor have the gospel preached to them" (Luke 7:22). When it comes to the Beatitudes (Matthew 5:2-11; Luke 6:20-23), Luke's "poor" differs in emphasis from Matthew's "poor in spirit." Matthew's have no counterpart to temporalize his spiritual meaning, whereas Luke immediately stakes his meaning to the temporal by pairing it later with a warning to the materially wealthy: "Woe to you who are rich."[3]

Again and again, Jesus returns to focus on these groups. He urges others to give to those who are poor, he elevates them, and he warns the rich.[4] These episodes reveal the importance of those who are poor and otherwise disadvantaged to Jesus. He ministers to them both in word, proclaiming to them the good news of the kingdom, and in deed, healing them and breaking bread together.

These themes were often worked out at table, either as parables or through tangible, physical examples from the life of Jesus. In nearly every major section of Luke's Gospel—from Jesus' early encounters with John the Baptist through his ascension—Jesus eats with others. In Luke 5, Jesus dines at Levi's house. In Luke 7, he accepts a Pharisee's invitation to a meal. In Luke 9, he provides and shares in a miraculous meal with five thousand. In Luke 11, he eats at another Pharisee's house. In Luke 22, he takes his last supper with his disciples. And even after his resurrection, Jesus breaks bread and eats fish with his disciples in Luke 24.[5] Meals permeate Luke's gospel. Jesus' choice of dinner company reinforced that the messianic message and ministry is for those who are poor.

Many of these meals run Jesus afoul of Jewish leadership. But in Luke 14, we get a special glimpse into how the kingdom transforms cultural practices that depart from divine design. These parables are "a signal of what is happening in the arrival of God's reign. Jesus' ministry is characterized by deep welcome and the invitation to eat together is extended to all people and is particularly offered to those at the margins."[6] God's table was wider than Jesus' first century audience could even think.

HEALING AND RUN-INS AT THE TABLE

A woman bent over and unable to fully straighten herself appears before Jesus in the synagogue on the Sabbath in Luke 13:11. This is Jesus' third time faced with the decision about whether to "do work"[7] on the Sabbath. He heals her and the synagogue leader who saw it becomes indignant, lecturing the people gathered not to come for healing on the Sabbath. Jesus rebukes him, however, calling him a hypocrite and putting him, and those with him, to shame (Luke 13:17). The ruler is brought low, while the woman who had needed healing is exalted.

Later, Jesus answers a question from the crowd about how many will be saved (Luke 13:23). Many will miss out on his kingdom, he explains, despite their claims to have eaten with him. He then concludes with a word on reversals: some are last who will be first and some are first who will be last (Luke 13:30). Good news for those who are last, less so for his current company.

In Luke 14, on yet another Sabbath, Jesus heads to the home of one of the rulers of the Pharisees, a popular Jewish sect at the turn of the century who considered themselves guardians of the Torah and enjoyed considerable social influence. This is the only documented invitation Jesus receives to a meal from a "ruler," making it possibly his most prestigious. Yet he shares it with a group with whom tensions already run high.

A man with visibly swollen limbs appears at the ruler's house, much like the earlier bent over woman at the synagogue. Perhaps he happens by, or perhaps he is planted. In either case, the Pharisees watch Jesus closely to see if he will heal again on the Sabbath (verse 1). Of course, he does not turn the man away, but heals him, a choice met predictably with displeasure (verse 4). Anticipating their objections, Jesus preempts his opponents, defending his actions and silencing them (verse 6). Based on the parallel passage in Luke 13, it's time for a word on kingdom reversals, a theme found within these two chapters. Jesus begins a series of banquet-themed parables where those who are poor and humble come to the fore (verse 7).

The Self-Interested Guests

Banquet guests scramble to claim the most honorable seats for themselves, playing a more composed game of musical chairs. Pharisees were well known for their "rapacity and occupation with social esteem."[8] In Matthew's woes to the scribes and Pharisees, Jesus charges them with loving places of honor at feasts and the best seats in the synagogues (Matthew 23:6). Although the prevailing Greco-Roman belief was that "honour is not honour unless publicly claimed, displayed and acknowledged,"[9] Jesus reminds them: "The greatest among you shall be your servant. Whoever exalts himself will be humbled and whoever humbles himself will be exalted" (Matthew 23:12). This was no doubt a hard teaching, as the appearance of honor was honor itself.

Jesus observes the scene unfolding before him at the ruler of the Pharisee's table and seizes this opportunity to teach (Luke 14:7). First, he condemns the dinner guest's selection of seats: "'Do not sit down in a place of honor, lest someone more distinguished than you be invited'" (verse 8). His instructions to take the lowest place so they could be elevated (verse 10) could've easily led them to simply reverse their strategy but toward the same end, so he clarifies: God will humble those who exalt themselves and exalt those who humble themselves (verse 11). Rather than being awarded by society, status is conferred by God.

In this parable, God is the true host who ultimately says, "Friend, move up higher" (verse 10). But also, as Jesus' teaching about the kingdom is self-revelatory, Jesus himself perfectly modeled the humility he suggests when he took the place of a servant and eschewed equality with God (Philippians 2:6-7), trusting his father to one day exalt him. On its face, it appears Jesus is saying that his followers should avoid places of honor. But by his example, Jesus redesignates the lowest place *as* the place of honor, the same seat taken by the king of the kingdom.

Symposia Literature

Parables do not stand on their own; rather, they draw meaning from their broader literary and social contexts. Luke 14's images, structure, and plot reached beyond a Jewish worldview for meaning; they were written and read within an environment heavily shaped by Greek culture. We all know Luke as a gospel and it includes parables as well. What is lost on modern readers is that Luke also contains portions in the style of symposium literature,[10] a favorite among Greeks.

Symposium literature recreated or mimicked conversations that happened at banquets after the meal.[11] These discussions covered philosophy, culture, and even proper banquet etiquette—like seating assignments. Luke employed this literary tradition.

Table Talk was a well-known work of symposia literature containing several dialogues dealing with seats of honor. Comparing its dialogues with Luke's parable illuminates what Luke attempts—and subverts—in his recounting of Jesus' words. One dialogue from *Table Talk* in particular touches on where the highest-ranked leaders sat in a room:

> Our inquiry fell upon the subject of the places at a banquet...different peoples hold different places in honour: the Persians the most central place, occupied by the king; the Greeks the first place; the Romans the last place on the middle couch, called the consul's place.[12]

In Christ's kingdom, the lowest place had been occupied by the highest ranked. The overlapping motifs and their treatment suggest both Plutarch and Luke rely on popular themes found within that tradition.[13] Plutarch uses these motifs to advance Greek values, but Luke uses them to clarify Christ, encouraging humility and the inclusion of unlikely banquet guests.

Luke flips the symposium on its head, "challenging the standard banqueting practices of the elite in the first-century Mediterranean World more generally,"[14] where humility is seen as a vice, not a virtue, and like dines with like.[15] In its place, he casts a beatific vision of a banquet consistent with the ethics and aims of Christ and his kingdom.

Greco-Roman and Jewish Banquet Culture

In both Greco-Roman and Jewish cultures, shared midday and evening meals had their own formalized rules of etiquette that helped define in-group borders and upheld socio-religious views of purity. Shared meals enhanced and reflected friendships and social networks. They provided opportunity for signaling and securing honor. Jesus found fault with their exclusivity and their prominent use to further one's own interests.

Luke may have been targeting the symposium by recounting Jesus' instructions to the guests and host, material unique to his gospel. The contrast between the behavior Jesus sees and what he advocates for at the ruler's house differentiates between the way of the culture and the way of his kingdom. Green observes that Jesus is not merely playing the sage, but rather, "he is toppling the familiar world of the ancient Mediterranean, overturning its socially constructed reality and replacing it with what must have been regarded as a scandalous alternative."[16] Jesus shows them what it would look like for his kingdom to come, on earth as it is in heaven.

THE SELF-INTERESTED HOST

Next Jesus turns his attention to the host: "When you give a dinner or a banquet, do not invite your friends or your brothers or your relatives or rich neighbors" (Luke 14:12). This practice was not only socially acceptable, but even encouraged—as his host must have done on this occasion. Even today, this is the norm. Our hustling for status and networking has ancient roots. The marginalized and outsiders may be just as unlikely to grace our tables as theirs. The Pharisees had peppered Jesus throughout his ministry with questions about many of his and his disciples' dining practices. Their preoccupation with who Jesus shared meals with reflected their own views about who qualified as acceptable beneficiaries of hospitality. "Because invitations served as currency in the marketplace of prestige and power, there is nothing extraordinary or particularly objectionable to the inclusion of one's social peers and family, persons from whom one could expect reciprocation."[17] To think otherwise would have been considered foolish. No good was freely given, not even from the gods.

Jesus initially casts repayment as undesirable and to be avoided. Given the culture, however, his audience would naturally not only welcome repayment but expect it. To not reciprocate would have been an affront. Instead, he urges them to invite those who are poor, those with disabilities, those who are blind, and those who are limping precisely because they cannot pay back. This would move their hospitality out of the realm of indirect self-interest and status-angling into radically countercultural generosity—a generosity more like his.

This type of hospitality took neither one's own status nor the status of the recipient into account and embraced a kind of giving most would consider a loss. Under the pervasive system of reciprocity, giving was a form of insurance, a way to establish networks of relationships you could turn to if you ran into trouble. Generosity to friends, be it in gifts or in hospitality, was your safety net. This is why banquets were such lavish affairs.[18]

THOSE WHO ARE POOR, THOSE WITH DISABILITIES, THOSE WHO ARE BLIND, AND THOSE WHO ARE LIMPING

On the other end of the social ladder were those who were poor. There was a category of those who were poor who worked to support themselves, primarily through agriculture. But those in Luke 14 were destitute—devoid of status, resources, and networks—and could only depend on the generosity of others to survive. These were not people who just barely made ends meet with nothing extra, but those who lived in abject poverty and only survived through begging.[19] With wealth being a sign of honor in antiquity, those in view in these parables, lacking wealth also lacked honor.

In Jesus' day, if you were disabled, you were likely also beggarly poor. In contrast with the abled poor, however, individuals with physical disabilities sometimes served special purposes at banquets. New Testament scholar Louise Gosbell notes,

Many people with physical anomalies were placed on display in order to satisfy the curiosity of eager onlookers. Both Greek and Roman philosophers include examples of people with unusual physical characteristics being displayed in both private and public settings...at banquets and public events such as the theatre and at gladiatorial battles.[20]

But the ostracizing came not only from Greeks and Romans. Jewish law prohibited individuals with physical disabilities from participating in temple worship and considered them ineligible for the priesthood (Leviticus 21:17-21). Not only were they excluded from religious life here and now, but some believed them shut out from the anticipated end times messianic banquet as well. The *Rule of the Congregation*, an important document of the Jewish Dead Sea community at the turn of the second century states,

> Everyone who is defiled in his flesh, paralyzed in his feet or in his hands, lame, blind, deaf, dumb or defiled in his flesh with a blemish visible to the eyes...these shall not enter to take their place among the congregation of famous men, for the angels of holiness are among their [congregation].[21]

Besides cleanliness issues, a prevailing view at the time was that disability was the result of sin (John 9:1-3). To the Jew, people with disabilities were unclean and were left out for fear of contamination. To the Gentile, they were a source of derision yet included to mock and reinforce a sense of superiority. In neither case were people with disabilities viewed or welcomed as equals.

As we've already discussed, those with physical disabilities often played the role specifically of "the uninvited," or *akletoi*, at banquets, "the uninvited member of the banquet who would entertain the invited guests."[22] They were subject to public mocking and ridicule. While not all *akletoi* had physical disabilities, they were the majority of this group. They were, of course, invited, but the entrenched tendency toward social stratification resulted in the formation of this "distinct social group that existed in association with the practice of banqueting and symposia. Their role as marginal, as 'other', their social inferiority to the real recipients of banquet invitations, is understood by all present at the banquet."[23]

By contrast, Jesus makes it clear in Luke 14 he means the identities of those marginalized groups literally because of their assumed inability to reciprocate the gesture. Moreover, they are to be *invited*, not serve as *akletoi*. By so doing, Jesus abolishes *quid pro quo* in his kingdom. "Standard patterns of reciprocity and concern for those of our own standing are overturned here."[24] Dressing up self-interest as generosity is incompatible with kingdom ethics, and indirect self-promotion is deviant in the new social system.

However, Jesus strikes at something deeper than a dinner invitation in this parable for the host: it's not that repayment is inherently bad—in verse 14 Jesus himself uses repayment as an incentive for inviting those who are poor—but that the repayment sought through one's own maneuvering is illicitly gained and short lived. To give in God's kingdom is to deliberately take a loss here in exchange for the promise of incalculable repayment later—as Christ did through his suffering. In that loss, we taste something of heaven—fellowship with our Messiah. The repayment offered by God is the real deal, the ultimate reward. And only his repayment lasts (Matthew 6:20). In this parable, not only does Jesus perfectly model inviting those who are poor and marginalized to join him at his table, but God is the true guest as well, for what is done for the least of these is done for him (Matthew 25:40).

Both the guests and the host at this meal fall under the same category:

currently exalted and looking to reap the full benefits of their worldly status now. They engaged in practices that secured, reinforced, and signaled their status and by extension their honor. At the end of the day, they sought either honor or repayment for themselves. To each, Jesus proposes the same "lesson": that which is conferred by heaven is of true value (verses 11, 14).

By contrast, the main characters in the parable in verses 15 through 24 have no such exalted status. "Luke shows a clear awareness that to deviate from physical, cognitive, or emotional norms is to stand at considerable social disadvantage."[25] In a setting where people are hyper-respecters of persons, Jesus instructs those currently exalted to do the opposite, to be like him, showing no partiality. He speaks not just of future kingdom demographics but shows how his reign disrupts in the present what was widely considered socially acceptable and went otherwise unchallenged. Luke 14 is meant as a corrective to a culture of inequality widespread and conspicuously displayed around the table. As the table went, so went the culture. But Christ's table brings the margins to the center, refuting the notion that they are dispensable, unworthy, or optional. A new standard for community is created in Christ among those who follow him and share in his table.[26]

THE GREAT BANQUET

Perhaps to break the tension, a guest exclaims, "Blessed is everyone who will eat bread in the kingdom of God," a phrase evoking the Beatitudes—who is blessed, and to whom the kingdom belongs. With that, Jesus begins a third parable.

A man prepares a great banquet and right before it's to begin, the original invitees all cancel, presenting a host of unconvincing excuses. Angered, the master of the house dispatches his servants to bring in those who are poor, those with disabilities, those who are blind, and those who are limping, and those who live in the outskirts of town to fill his home. (In that day, the further one lived from the center of town, the less well-off they were socioeconomically.) The banquet is ultimately enjoyed by those of humble estate, by those who are poor and outcasts. It's not that they enter solely because of their social status or disability. No, they enter the kingdom the same way all do, by accepting the invitation. There is a space at the table for them, they are given the dignity of receiving an invitation from the king; the kingdom belongs even to such as these who, to the world, lack anything to commend themselves. By contrast, those most anticipating it, who assume they will share in it, taste nothing of it.

LAST WILL BE FIRST AND THE FIRST WILL BE LAST

There is a deep irony that the Pharisees, concerned with self-promotion and trapping Jesus in this scene, eat at the table with Jesus and yet have no part in his "banquet." The man with dropsy, though, as the recipient of healing, goes away having tasted the fruit of the kingdom. Just as those who are poor are not taken figuratively in Jesus' instructions to the host, neither are they figurative in the parable of the master.

For the key to this parable, we look back to its parallel passage in chapter 13: "Some are last who will be first, and some are first who will be last." Those at table with Jesus were invited, but receiving their honor and repayment now, will be last. Those who are poor and the uninvited *akletoi,* who lack honor and resources now, will be first and enjoy the bread of the feast.

This parable makes both social and religious points by including at the banquet those who are poor, those with disabilities, those who are blind, and those who are limping, and those living on highways and hedges. It is both social and religious because Jesus is showing that the social *is* religious. His kingdom was meant to reorder our approach to status, honor, relationships, and even hospitality. We see the kingdom reversals at work in the transposition of status: the humble are exalted and the exalted are humbled. But we also see it in un-invitable being invited.

A literal interpretation of these "un-invitable" groups also forces us to reckon with our treatment of them. The church today doesn't fare much better than the Gentiles or Jews in Jesus' time. Braun points out,

> Far from being people whom one should include in one's community, regard as friends, and care for when in need, people with disabilities were often objects of scorn, shame, and absurd comedy. Moreover, this tendency, though not as overt as in the ancient world, still lurks in our own context.[27]

Those who are poor and those with disabilities continue to be othered, neglected, or tokenized and face, within church walls, visibility and accessibility issues. They remain the "them" of the pews, special projects, or charity, but not the "us" of our dinner tables and homes.

THE END OF STATUS MEETS THE BEGINNING OF MERCY

Some scholars have seen the groups Jesus called out in these parables as a proxy for Gentiles, showing the kingdom is not exclusive to the Jews. However, this overlooks the very people Jesus sought to honor. Instead, in Luke 14:1-24, Jesus outlaws the rampant status-chasing common within the broader culture and elevates those of lowly estate. In challenging the very idea of social hierarchy, Jesus was not doing something new, but reviving something that had been lost: "The original meaning of the Messianic feast in the Hebrew Scriptures."[28] The parable of the great banquet speaks to both the social and religious inclusivity of God's kingdom. Including those who are poor, those with disabilities, those who are blind, and those who are limping as guests— in addition to those rounded up from the highways and hedges after the initial invitees cancel—highlights that the kingdom subverts the practice of securing, reinforcing, or signaling social position. In God's kingdom, both the uninvited and the un-invitable have a place at the table. This is good news not only for those who are poor and outcasts, but also for the exalted in desperate need of liberation from the tyranny of status chasing. His kingdom was a kingdom of reversals.

Jesus offered to put an end to the status-bound, socially accepted, self-aggrandizing ways of navigating society. Jesus has a specific mission to those who are poor and, in very real ways, understanding and living out the first two parables enables us to align ourselves fully with the kingdom's focus on those who are poor, those who are disabled, and outcasts.

Wouldn't it be transformational to live without concern for status? What a fuller picture it would paint for an onlooking world if we lived socially upside-down lives. To be that free. To share our lives and not just the gospel with the otherwise uninvited. What comfort to know that wherever you fall in the eyes of the world is no indication of where you fall in the eyes of your Father. And what a challenge to pursue socially diverse and inclusive friendships, and for our homes and churches to more closely reflect this feast.

Is there still a sense in which the believer today who is not disabled can benefit from assuming the perspective of those who are poor, those with disabilities, those who are blind, and those who are limping of this parable? Absolutely. Heritage and status do not make you shoo-ins for God's kingdom. We don't put our trust in those things for entry. Instead, we accept Jesus' invitation to come, not letting our pursuit of the things of the world keep us away. We live out of the knowledge we are a people who have been given a free gift we can never repay. If we ever wrestle with feeling status-deficient, we can know the work of Christ on the cross evened out the status curve in the kingdom and there's no *quid pro quo*.

But there's also benefit from understanding the implications of these words being spoken to those who are poor and socially marginalized. Our Lord welcomed the uninvited and outcast as honored guests as his table. To truly understand his heart and ministry, we must go and do likewise.

LITURGY FOR INCLUSION

Exalted Caller of the Least, we thank you:
for turning your divine eye toward us,
for accommodating our inability to see rightly, hear rightly,
walk rightly, or offer you anything of value in return.
We come to you in need.

We come in wonder at our inclusion;
we come in wonder at the extravagance of your table,
and at the attentiveness of your servants
who make us feel at home here, as equals, as no less worthy.
For you have assembled the unworthy.

Our tears have been our food;
we are the desperate and disdained of the world.
What we could never dream of attaining here, we have in you:
we have no home but yours,
no honor but what you confer,
no reward but that which we shall receive at the raising of the
just,
and in this we indeed have more than enough;
treasures too plentiful for words.

Exalted Caller of the Least,
May we be forever open to your invitation,
eager to be filled from the storehouses of your grace,
not willing to forego your invitation to tend to the things of
this world;
or hesitating to come because we've been deceived into
believing ourselves inferior.

Grant us the ability to see right, hear right, and walk right
so we may remit only this in return:
that should we be given the opportunity
to offer others a foretaste of what we ourselves have here
savored,
we would likewise hold nothing back,
see none as beneath us,
silence not the pained cries for mercy,
seek neither for ourselves honor nor repayment,
and that we would,
with great joy and gladness,
and immeasurable gratitude,
offer others what you've offered us:
the opening wide of your ever welcoming doors.

Chapter 10

FEAST FOR THE RETURNED PRODIGAL

To the Lost

> *The father said to his servants, "Bring quickly the best robe,*
> *and put it on him, and put a ring on his hand, and shoes on*
> *his feet. And bring the fattened calf and kill it, and let us eat*
> *and celebrate. For this my son was dead, and is alive again;*
> *he was lost, and is found." And they began to celebrate.*
>
> LUKE 15:22-24

The parable of the lost sons (Luke 15:11-30) enjoys almost unparalleled recognition among the parables of Jesus. It is a rhapsodic variation on now familiar themes: more broadly, on Luke's theme of reversal we saw in the previous chapter, and more immediately, as the final installment in a trilogy of parables (Luke 15:1-7, 8-10, 11-30) about the recovery and celebration of that which was lost. Though popularly known as the parable of the prodigal son, both sons, as we shall see, are lost. And to both, the father says, "Come, feast."

The Gospels portray the repentance of sinners as central to Jesus' messianic mission. Jesus declares, in Luke 5:32, he has "not come to call the righteous but the sinners to repentance." Whatever else he may do for sinners—feed them, heal them, teach them—is all aimed at their repentance, without which they would fail to enter the kingdom that has come and is coming.

Tax Collectors and Sinners

The two introductory verses of Luke 15 provide scaffolding for the entire chapter. Upon seeing tax collectors and sinners flock to Jesus, the Pharisees and scribes grumble that Jesus attracts, welcomes, and even eats with those they consider religious deadbeats. They draw near to him, and Jesus does nothing to discourage it. The parables of the lost sheep, lost coin, and lost sons are Jesus' response.

This is neither the first nor the last time such an accusation will be lobbied at Jesus or his disciples. Throughout the Gospel of Luke, they are criticized for whom they befriend and with whom they dine. In Luke 5:30, the Pharisees and scribes question the disciples when Jesus accepts an invitation to feast at the home of Levi, the tax collector. In Luke 7:39, they again lambast him for letting a sinful woman cry over, kiss, and anoint his feet. In Luke 19, when he dines with Zacchaeus, a chief tax collector, they grumble, "He has gone in to be the guest of a man who is a sinner" (Luke 19:7).

The Pharisees' objection to these groups arose from their respective orientations toward the Law. Where Pharisees were law-abiding, tax collectors and sinners were seen as lawless. They were the exact opposite of those to whom the Pharisees believed the kingdom belonged, and they lived in open defiance of the Law the Pharisees strove to preserve and uphold. They were notoriously immoral. As Craig Blomberg puts it, "'Sinners' in this context refers to those who flagrantly violated the cultural and religious norms of Judaism."[1] The gospel according to the Pharisees was that the kingdom did not belong to such sinners, but to the scrupulous. In striking contrast, Jesus praised the sinner who anointed his feet in Luke 7 and declared, "Her sins, which are many, are forgiven—for she loved much. But he who is forgiven little, loves little" (Luke 7:47). By this calculus, sinners always have an advantage when it comes to loving Jesus.

The sociopolitical climate of the day also exacerbated the Pharisees' disdain for tax collectors. On top of employing corrupt means to collect more customs and duties from their own people than were due, Jewish tax collectors worked for Rome, the enemy. So in addition to being dishonest Law-breakers, they were also seen as traitors. They may have been people of some means, but they were considered outsiders all the same. Yet in Luke 18, before the smug and contemptuous, Jesus made himself clear: the tax collector who cried for mercy from God went away justified, not the Pharisee enamored with his own religious accomplishments. These could not justify him.

The question of whether the Jews' Messiah could be a friend to sinners sprang from the Pharisees' views on salvation. The Pharisees trusted in painstaking observance of the Law—albeit mixed with the "tradition of men" (Matthew 15:1-20; Mark 7:1-23; Luke 11:37-41)—to remain in good standing before God as his covenant people. Ongoing and public failures would have disqualified tax collectors and sinners from salvation and its benefits, despite their Jewish heritage. The Pharisees spoke and lived as though the exacting obedience to the Law they considered faithfulness entitled them to the kingdom. In their view, tax collectors and sinners were not just the lost of Israel, but irrecoverable. Pharisees saw them as "people who have been left to themselves, the sheep that have no Shepherd who were no longer looked upon as belonging to the true people of God."[2] They had no part in the family.

Defending his choice to dine with Zacchaeus, Jesus says in Luke 19:10, "The Son of Man came to seek and to save the lost." He alludes to Ezekiel 34:4, where the prophet accuses Israel's religious leaders of not bringing back stray sheep or searching for the lost. Although they were the objects of the Pharisees' scorn, the lost were the very objects of Jesus' mercy, welcome, and mission. Ezekiel goes on to share these words from God, "Behold, I, I myself will search for my sheep and seek them out...I will seek the lost" (verses 11, 16). "How could Jesus be a friend to sinners?" the Pharisees wondered, yet it was for none but sinners he had come.

THE LOST SHEEP AND THE LOST COIN

The conflict above sets the stage for the parables that follow, each shedding light on why Jesus gladly received sinners and ate with them. The first two of them, the parables of lost sheep and lost coin, are relatively straightforward and share an identical structure of loss, search, recovery, and feast: something is lost and its owner searches for it, finds it, and celebrates its recovery. Both end with a lesson: just as the owners rejoice over finding what was lost, heaven rejoices over the repentant.

In each of these parables, we are thrust into the main character's shoes and introduced to what's lost. In the parable of the lost sheep, Jesus asks "'What man of you...'" (Luke 15:4) and for the parable of the lost coin, he asks "'What woman of you...'" (Luke 15:8). The sheep is one of a hundred whereas the coin, worth about a days' wages, is one of only ten, an escalation that perhaps hints at the loss being more keenly felt. Next, we see the search—the shepherd bolts, leaving 99 behind, shepherdless in the open country, to go look for the one. The woman lights the lamps, sweeps the house, and seeks diligently. Both lost items are recovered, the sheep even hoisted over the shepherd's shoulder and carried home. Both call together their friends and neighbors saying, "Rejoice with me" and together celebrate the recovery of what was lost.

Consider the drastic lengths to which these characters go to get back what most would consider not worth the effort. To leave 99 percent of your sheep in the open country to look for one just didn't make sense. It would have to be one extraordinary sheep, but we aren't given that information. Craig Blomberg notes, "'Parallels' to these two parables in the ancient Mediterranean world consistently alleviate this tension by making the lost sheep or coin worthy of special attention."[3] Jesus, however, leaves the tension be. He makes no effort to resolve it by ascribing any special worth to the lost item that would justify the search and rescue effort or celebration thereafter. Rather, he draws us into a story about one unconventionally generous father.

THE LOST SONS

"Which one of you, having two sons, if one has run away, does not keep watch for his return. And at first sight of his shadow, he runs out to greet him, embracing and kissing him, and throwing on him precious vestments and ornaments of sonship and honor, rejoicing. And when he comes home, he calls together his friends and neighbors, killing the fattened calf and saying, 'Rejoice with me, let us eat and celebrate, for I have found my son who was lost.' Just so, I tell you, there is unbridled joy in heaven over one sinner who repents."

This is the parable of the prodigal son we didn't get.

Instead, we get a gritty version full of scandal, betrayal, family drama, and tension. We encounter the brutal world alongside him, feeling his shame at the depths to which he's plunged. We get to know the father and experience the generosity and gentleness he lavishes upon both his sons. We feel the relief and joy he feels at his younger son's safe return. And we get to hear from the "ninety-nine," the child who never strayed and had no need of repentance. We feel his slight at the extravagant welcome his brother receives. We get all this while still following the general structure of loss, search, recovery, and feast.

WE ARE FAMILY

Jesus' decision to set this story within a family is intentional. Family language is covenant language. Sonship in particular is "the realization of the promise of the New Covenant, the continuation and fulfillment of the bond between the Lord and Israel." [4] It also implies a web of relationships: each son is not only a son but also a brother, embedded in a larger extended family and community.

You don't have to travel that far back in history to see where the actions of one family member could bring shame to all. What first comes to my mind is *Pride and Prejudice* and the sullied reputation the entire Bennet family anticipates when Lydia Bennet recklessly runs off with a soldier. Nor do you have to travel far around the world to find places where such collectivism governs conduct today.

The Younger Son: "I am no longer worthy."

The younger son infamously asks his father for his share of the inheritance early. He's tired of home and eager to spread his wings. According to the laws of inheritance, he was entitled to one-third of the estate (Deuteronomy 21:17).

Even if not illegal, his request was impudent and relationship damaging. This was no way to honor one's father. It turned a family relationship transactional. What's more, his actions had broader consequences: "Everyone in the family, including the lowest slave, is poorer as soon as the younger son leaves with his part of the family inheritance."[5] Yet his father graciously concedes, and soon the youngster has liquidated his property and set out for a faraway country in search of independence and pleasure.

Just as he burns through the last of his inheritance, a severe famine strikes the land, aggravating his already precarious situation. In his desperation, he goes to work for a Gentile tending pigs. Beyond the deep shame and dishonor this carried since pigs were considered unclean, it would have further distanced him from his community. According to Jewish oral law, raising pigs was forbidden to Jews.[6] Between working for a Gentile and his pig gig, he had sunk to an unimaginably new low.

No one—not a soul—will give him even a single bite to eat, and his situation becomes so dire that he finds himself craving pig feed. Stunned by the devastating lack of generosity and mocked by an empty stomach, it occurs to him that even his father's hired servants are better off than he. While they have their fill of bread, he wastes away. Independence was fast losing its luster.

The grumble of his stomach jolted him back to himself, and he began to contemplate returning home. He decides to go confess and plead for mercy from his father. He's even content to be taken back as a hired servant—a position lower than a slave with far less stability—since he believes himself no longer worthy to live as a son. Broken, resolved, and repentant, he begins the journey home.

The Father: "Let us eat and celebrate."

The Old Testament gave instructions about how to treat rebellious sons. This wasn't it. A rebellious son unresponsive to discipline should be brought before the city elders at the entrance gate to his home to be publicly shamed and stoned to death (Deuteronomy 21:18-21).

I wonder if a single day had gone by since the son left that the father hadn't hoped for his return, perhaps keeping watch at the edge of his property. How many false alarms had he had, thinking it was his son, only to find some random passerby? Not this time. As soon as he could make out it was his son, he bounded after him full of compassion and an affection undiminished by time or the circumstances surrounding his departure.

Joy, joy—pure joy! My son, returned! Before a word of his son's prepared speech can escape his lips, the father showers him with kisses and wraps him in a tight embrace. Up close, he could see the wear and tear of the far country etched all over his son's frame. This wasn't the reception the son, or Jesus' audience, would have imagined. He is rushed by grace. Instead of censure or shame from the father, we get relief and joy.

His paternal instincts produced "not a pointed finger but open arms."[7] Instead of withholding his welcome until the son demonstrates he's changed, the father unleashes it without strings when merely letting him live would have been kind enough. There was nothing to prove or repay, only to receive. He did not have to promise never to run off again to earn his father's welcome or kindness. Maybe he changes, maybe he doesn't. The passage never says. The options on the table were death or servitude, and the father chooses "honored son of mine."

My senior year of high school, I totaled my mother's car. I flipped it over a guardrail one rainy December afternoon trying to take an exit at the last second. It rolled to a stop in a ditch and I thought to myself after returning right side up that my mother was going to kill me. I hadn't gotten permission to go where I was going (though I'd gotten it to drive somewhere else). But when I finally spoke with her, she just wanted to know I was okay. The day after, at church, she rose to share the news with her Sunday school class that I'd been in a potentially fatal car crash and escaped with a cut on my pinky. For Christmas that year, she even gifted me with a huge box of my favorite candies that had been thrown from the car, along with everything else, when the windows shattered. I had made an incredibly costly mistake, I had exercised poor judgment, and I was mentally prepared to beg, barter, or work my way back into her good graces. But none of that was required. I got from my mother, instead, the same kind of welcome as this son.

The younger son begins to recite his speech, confessing his sin and stating he's no longer worthy to be called his son. Before he has a chance to propose becoming a hired servant, though, his father cuts him off. This was not a day for sadness or self-pity, but for joy. The father orders his servants to quickly bring out the best robe, a ring, and sandals for his child's bare, journey-worn feet. These gifts were about reinstating the son in both word and in deed, allaying his feelings of shame and unworthiness with gestures that shouted, "You belong," "You are no less my son," and "You are forgiven." Though anticipating shame and a demotion, he is greeted with unequivocal signs of honor. From dreary depths, the younger son was lifted to unimaginably high heights.

Finally, the father orders the fattened calf be killed so they can celebrate. The feast was an expression of the father's unrestrained joy over his receiving his son back from the dead safe and sound (Luke 15:24, 27, 32). In first-century Palestine, the presence of meat alone signified a special meal, while a fattened calf was usually reserved for major religious holidays. It was as if the father was declaring the son's return a holiday, given the amount of preparation required for such a celebration.[8] The father's display is so ostentatious there can be no doubt in the son's mind his honor is restored and there is nothing for him to repay but only to live as a son. MacLaren ponders,

> I question whether forgiveness is ever true which is not, like God's, attended by large-hearted gifts. If pardon is only the non-infliction of penalty, then it is natural enough that it should be considered sufficient by itself, and that the evildoer should not be rewarded for having been bad. But if pardon is the outflow of the love of the offended to the offender, then it can scarcely be content with simply giving the debtor his discharge, and turning him into the world penniless. And, that being so, that love cannot stay its working until it has given all that it can bestow or we can receive. He always gives when He forgives.[9]

When we sin and fall short, we hope for the kind of large-hearted, love-sprung forgiveness offered by this father. But, like the younger son, we don't always expect it. Our stories may be less dramatic than his, yet they still resonate with his. Who of us has not failed? Who has not craved independence or been lured away by the pull of far-off lands? Who has not been held hostage by selfish ambition? The message for all of us is the same: "Go to God, and He will smile away your sin, and His forgiving love will melt the stains and the evil, as the sun this morning drank up the mists."[10] Even if our neighbors cannot help but treat us as our sins deserve, our Father does not. He is merciful and gracious, slow to anger, and abounding in steadfast love—all characteristics that invite repentance and reconciliation. His grace is a longer shot than we can even imagine, yet it is ours all the same.

THE ELDER SON: "THESE MANY YEARS I HAVE SERVED YOU."

The cycle of lost, sought, recovery, and feast restarts with the elder brother. As he nears home from working in the field, he overhears a live band and the sound of dancing. Perhaps he can even smell meat cooking from a distance. He calls for a servant to find out the occasion and learns his younger brother is back and his father has thrown a feast in honor of his safe return. Curiosity turns to furor. Outside, he stews and sulks for a while before his father goes out to search for him.

The elder son unleashes his indignation on his father, seeking to justify himself by reminding him of his pristine record. He must have thought that, to some extent, his father's generosity could be earned. He decries the unfairness of his brother's reception: "These many years I have served you, and I never disobeyed your command, yet you never gave me a young goat that I might celebrate with my friends" (Luke 15:29). His strict obedience to his father made him feel entitled to special treatment. It wasn't that his father didn't give him a fatted calf; it was that *despite all his work for his father,* he didn't *even* get a skinny goat.

It's ironic that the elder son claims obedience in the very moment he disobeys his father's entreaty to join him in welcoming his brother. He becomes an outsider, not due to any stinginess of his father, but due to his own inability to see himself as lost and his father's grace as good.

A focus on behavior, not motives, caused him to overlook his sin. This made him slow to confess, slow to forgive, and slow to receive forgiveness. And those forgiven little, love little, and make little of grace. The obedient one rejects grace in favor of reward-seeking and gets neither. Should he only repent, the floodgates of grace would open once more to sweep him up in a most joyous celebration.

Like the younger son, the elder son felt insufficient before his father—not because of the wrong he'd done, but because the good he had done wasn't good enough. Unlike the younger son, who thought his behavior *disqualified* him from sonship, the older son believed his *qualified* him. What he really needed to hear was, "Stop working; you *belong*. Make yourself at home in my grace."

The elder brother had forgotten he was a son. His choice of the words *served* and *command* evoked a relationship of servitude rather than family. Neither wasting nor working for our inheritance honors the father. What the father attempts to communicate to each is the same: sonship isn't earned.

Next, the elder brother distances himself from his younger brother, calling him "this son of yours" (Luke 15:30). He brings up sin already repented for and compares what his tainted brother was given with what he was denied. Not only had his obedience made him entitled, but it had also made him proud. C.S. Lewis writes, "It is the comparison that makes you proud: the pleasure of being above the rest. Once the element of competition has gone, pride has gone."[11] Repentance requires humility, without which the doors to the feast, as it were, would remain effectively closed.

It's his broken relationship with his father that ultimately keeps the elder son from a restored relationship with his brother. The father nudges him toward reconciliation not by downplaying his younger son's failings, but by highlighting the father-son relationship: "My son, you are always with me, and all that is mine is yours" (Luke 15:31).

This should have been the basis for welcoming his brother back. The father has been gracious to him, too, a fact he seems to forget. "The elder should not lose sight of the benefits he has always had because of his access to the father. In a sense, he has always had access to the celebration. The animals are his!"[12] Had he believed that to be true, there would have been no sense of competition with the brother, no comparison of their treatment. His contempt for his brother was rooted in what he believed he deserved. But how could one who already possessed all that belonged to the father suffer lack?

The father reminds him it's not just his son they received back, but that he received back a brother. He also affirms it was right and necessary to celebrate. To feel self-pity or indignation instead of joy, then, was not simply bull-headed, but wrong. The one who wasn't lost, who was righteous and had no need of repentance, had cut himself off from the father's grace precisely because he felt entitled to it. Psychologist and counselor Edward Welch writes,

> The character of God is the basis for our connection to him, not our intrinsic worth. Self-worth, or anything we think would make us acceptable to God, would suit our pride but it has the disturbing side-effect of making the cross of Jesus Christ less valuable. If we have worth in ourselves, there is no reason to connect to the infinite worth of Jesus and receive what he has done for us.[13]

Grace always flows from the good pleasure of the father, not the worthiness of the son.

LOST AND FOUND

There's no third category in these parables. You're either lost or you're found. You're dead or alive. You're with the father or you're estranged. Both rebellion and self-righteousness are death. To repent of these is life.

There's no "ninety-nine righteous," either. For all fall short (Romans 3:23), none is righteous (Romans 3:10), there is none who does good, no not one (Romans 3:12). Isaiah 53:6 says, "All we like sheep have gone astray; we have turned—every one—to his own way." We are all stuck in the lost-sought-recovery-feast loop, save the self-righteous who resist recovery and miss the feast. In all our drifting and open rebellion, in all our striving after what is freely ours, God seeks us. And when we come to him, foul though we be, he and the angels rejoice.

There is, however, one who had no need of repentance, who was abandoned by his shepherd in the open country, and that is Christ. Christ knows what it is to be shamed (Luke 18:32). He knows what it is to be bogged down with the weight of *our* sin, for the Lord not only "laid on him the iniquity of us all" (Isaiah 53:6), but made him sin itself (2 Corinthians 5:21). He also knows the agony of being forsaken and judged by the father (Matthew 27:46). All that we might become truly righteous, not having a righteousness of our own, but that which comes through faith in him (Philippians 3:9). What a wonderful unburdening!

What the Pharisees meant as an insult about Jesus was actually high praise. What other savior would stoop so low? It does not debase Jesus to associate with sinners. Quite the contrary; it is part of his glory. The Most High associates with the most low. What makes for the splendor of the savior makes for our beauty as well, as recipients of his forgiveness and as those who get to grow in his likeness, loving and forgiving in these same ways. John Preston writes, "For there is nothing more effective to heal a rebellious heart...than to be persuaded that he shall be shown mercy and that his sins shall be forgiven in Christ."[14] This is precisely what these parables show. Jesus does not simply tolerate sinners; no, he throws big bashes for them when they return. He does not force them to grovel, but he gives them his best.

As Christ is formed more and more in us, we do the same. Amy

Carmichael put it well: "If I cast up a confessed, repented, and forsaken sin against another, and allow my remembrance of that sin to color my thinking and feed my suspicions, then I know nothing of Calvary love."[15] We do not dangle the sins of the repentant over them. We do not browbeat people with their confessed sins after we are supposed to have forgotten them; but we remember Calvary and how we're treated by God because of it. And then, we give them our best welcome. We invite others to the feast of which we ourselves are honored guests.

BROTHERS AND SONS

Both our ability to repent and to forgive hinge on seeing ourselves as who we really are. British Anglican minister Michael Ovey writes, "Repentance is a recognition of one's true identity."[16] Both sons had forgotten they were brothers. Both brothers had forgotten they were sons. Neither wasting our inheritance nor trying to work for what's already ours honors the father. MacLaren writes,

> Of the men that go for ever roaming with a hungry heart,
> through all the regions of life separate from God; and
> whether they seek their nourishment in the garbage of
> the sty, or whether fastidiously they look for it in the
> higher nutriment of mind and intellect and heart, still
> are condemned to be unfilled.[17]

Because we are often guilty of roaming through all regions as well, our need to repent stays constant. If that sounds daunting, if perhaps you had the thought, *Is my whole life supposed to be repentance?* the cross reveals the depth of our need.

As children of God, we can choose to be embittered siblings or we can take after our Father, responding to repentance with rejoicing, soothing instead of magnifying others' shame. When others repent, have a change of heart, feel convicted about something we've long mastered or never struggled with, do we join the feast, pout outside, or point fingers? Do we grab them a robe or put them on probation? We resemble the elder brother when we show disdain for the very riches of God's grace and kindness that lead people to repentance and act as though they must earn their place at the table. This parable reminds us we didn't earn ours.

Regardless of which son we identify with, the solution to our lostness is grace. The father seeks, invites, and rejoices at our return. He searches until we are found. When we remember this, repentance becomes a prelude to a feast, not an indelible mark of mortification.

Rebellious child, you have been justified. Even if your only option is to appear before God barefoot, disheveled, and full of shame, he will take you back because he is forgiving and generous. We don't work our way back into grace after failure. It's freely and joyously given. Shame may try to obstruct the way home, whispering, "Hide yourself, dodge rejection, lower your expectations." But heed instead the voice of the Father, for he will heal your waywardness and love you with abandon.

Self-righteous child, you have been justified. Do not submit again to a yoke of slavery. Your Father comes after you, too, and wants you to share in his joy. When you repent of your efforts to work for his love, he will call for the robe, the ring, and the sandals, and he will welcome you with a feast at your return just as he did for his younger son. Don't settle for servitude when you have sonship. Sonship in Christ is about being called out of slavery and servitude, not into it. Repent and live, and hear the Father pronounce over you the words that he spoke over his youngest, "My son was dead and is alive, was lost and has been found. Let us eat and celebrate."

LITURGY FOR PARDON

Most Generous Father, I come.
I come, at last, I come.
I have wasted my inheritance.
Chased after death,
yet when I found it, recoiled,
having expected life.

Lured into servitude unbecoming your child,
by a paradise promising everything,
giving nothing, taking all,
I ventured from your path.
But I was quickened by your hidden grace
that scours the far country for strays.

Homeward it took me,
though my feet felt the guide;
spit from the belly of a world too brutal for me,
with naught but shame and spent embers of hope,
I turned the corner home.

What welcome at your gates I meet,
these garments of sonship unearned,
a happiness to see me well,
a love more deep than my stain.

And of your gift of homesickness—
that ache revealing to me.

My Father, my inheritance,
to this I owe my seat.

Most Generous Father,
I have profaned our relationship
by living as a slave
rather than as a son
with unrestricted access
to all that is yours.

Vain, vain my toiling for what cannot be earned,
yet I deride those whose toil lags.
Unmoved by your grace, but addicted to wages,
I've been reluctant to come,
forgetting that the death I'm owed
was the death that you diverted.

My soul leaps and twirls at your words of pardon,
of ten million words none are as sweet as these:
you are faithful, just, forgiving,
not dealing as my sins deserve,
but embracing me with mercy.
Far you've removed my sin from me,
blotting out their faintest trace,
no condemnation remains,
no accusation stands.

Most Generous Father, I thank you;
and now, at last, we feast.

Chapter 11

BODY, BLOOD, BREAD, WINE

To the Church

*This feast is a spiritual table, at which Christ communicates
himself with all his benefits to us, and gives us there to
enjoy both himself and the merits of his sufferings and
death: nourishing, strengthening, and comforting our
poor comfortless souls, by the eating of his flesh, quickening
and refreshing them by their drinking of his blood.*

BELGIC CONFESSION

Another Sunday. Another table minimally dressed and topped with bread, small cups of wine or juice, a chalice or two. The pastor stands to instruct his flock in the deep meaning of the table before them. He finishes and heads bow as the elements are blessed. A time of personal reflection begins and once again, you sit in silence and wonder, *What's everyone else thinking about? When's it my turn? Will I see so-and-so in the line today?*

This is me many, if not most, Sundays we take communion, struggling in the 45 seconds of reflection we have to focus, unsure what I should even focus on. The Lord's table is about so much and yet the time to reflect on it so short. But then again, how much time would even be enough? Can I, with these few seconds, properly prepare for what's about to take place?

The Synoptic Gospels each contain explicit references to Jesus' last meal with his disciples just before he was betrayed. The words, "Do this in remembrance of me" (Luke 22:19) harken back to where the feasts began—with Passover, as though God were giving another *zik-karon*, memorial day, to his church. While we often frame communion as a meal of remembrance, memory alone doesn't encompass all this sacred table is about.

If there's anything we've learned about God and his meals with and for us, it's that, while they are about remembering, they're rarely *only* about remembering. In fact, they're never only about remembering. Those just aren't the kinds of feasts God throws. His feasts situate us properly in our present and tune our hearts to a future key. They affirm dear truths of his kingdom. They are respite, thanksgiving, and strength. They're participatory, formative, communal, covenantal. Heavy on mercy, kaleidoscopes of grace. This meal is no different. It's the most important, most nutrient-dense meal of our week.

THE NIGHT HE WAS BETRAYED

Communion is a multipurpose meal. It celebrates God's presence among his people while savoring it. It's the true Passover by which we were freed. This meal deepens our union with Christ and with our fellow believers. We take special care at this table to remember Christ's death and resurrection, and all its benefits, and to participate in the fellowship we have with him and each other.

Gathered in an upper room, the disciples prepare for the Passover. At some point in the meal, Jesus gets everyone's attention, side chatter stops, and the mood turns serious. He has something important to say. This meal is a special one, one different from others they'd shared, one he'd longed to eat with them before he no longer had the chance. He said, "I have earnestly desired to eat this Passover meal with you before I suffer. For I tell you I will not eat it again until it is fulfilled in the kingdom of God" (Luke 22:15-16).

This Is My Body Given for You

Jesus takes the bread and blesses it: "This is my body, which is given for you" (Luke 22:19). This wasn't the first time Jesus had referred to himself as bread. The day after he miraculously fed the five thousand, some among the crowd that had eaten their fill found him and asked him for a sign, like the one given to their forefathers who ate bread from heaven in the wilderness. Jesus corrected them: "Truly, truly, I say to you, it was not Moses who gave you the bread from heaven, but my Father gives you the true bread from heaven. For the bread of God is he who comes down from heaven and gives life to the world." Slow to catch his meaning, they ask him to give them that bread and Jesus responds with that well-known self-declaration, "I am the bread of life; whoever comes to me shall not hunger, and whoever believes in me shall never thirst" (John 6:35). He continues, "If anyone eats of this bread, he will live forever. And the bread that I will give for the life of the world is my flesh" (verse 51).

Jesus packed several astounding claims in those words. He offered them bread superior to the manna the Israelites had eaten in the desert. For 40 years, every morning God blanketed the face of the wilderness with flake-like bread, that they might believe he had delivered them. Exodus 16:8 records they got "bread to the full." As they gathered, all had what they needed—the one who had gathered much, not too much, and the one who had gathered little, not too little. There was neither surplus nor lack, just as had been with eating the Passover lamb. It was distributed among the people perfectly. Mention of manna evokes both Passover and Sukkot, as the exodus led Israel to the wilderness and Sukkot remembered God's provision for them there. Jesus, the bread who came by God into the world, by contrast, was so filling he needed only be eaten once and would drive away hunger for good. Thomas à Kempis wrote,

> Be thou favorable unto me, O merciful Jesus, and grant to me thy poor needy creature, sometimes at least in this holy communion to feel if it be but a small portion of thy hearty affectionate love, that my faith may become more strong, my hope in thy goodness may be increased, and that charity once perfectly inflamed, after the tasting of heavenly manna, may never die.[1]

Jesus was not bread adequate for the day, but bread adequate for all time, sent from heaven, giving life to the world. If anyone partook of his flesh by eating the bread, they would live forever, full. Jesus surpassed manna in every way: preeminently satisfying, sufficient for eternity, and animating the soul.

As Jesus approaches John the Baptist in John 1:29, John says, "Behold, the Lamb of God, who takes away the sin of the world!" In his identification as the lamb, Christ's flesh was given for the world and its sin. He, the Passover lamb, was slain to spare from judgment and death whoever would apply his blood to their doorposts. Beyond just sparing people, though, Jesus' sacrifice would also remove their sin, and through the giving of his body on the cross sanctify them (Hebrews 10:10).

So we sit with this, with the weight of living up to the demands of the Law lifted off our shoulders. Where previously we would have been condemned, because he was sacrificed in our stead, we live. We did not get what our sins deserved but got clemency. Because Jesus died, we don't just live, but we live free, not captive to our needs for physical pleasure, possessions, pride, or accomplishments. We live being home-grown by the Spirit. We live forgiven and seen by God through the lens of the perfect sacrifice of his Son given on our behalf. Our times of cowering, hiding, and slaving away are over. Backbreaking labor for acceptance has come to an end. We no longer need to worry about not measuring up. We were saved, so we can stop trying to save ourselves.

This Cup Is the New Covenant in My Blood

Jesus introduces the cup by saying it is the blood of the covenant—or, in Luke, the new covenant—which is poured out for many for the forgiveness of sins (Matthew 26:28; Mark 14:24; Luke 22:20). Covenant meals are common throughout the Bible and the Ancient Near East. Some of the best examples of these are the meal in Exodus 24, the Lord's Supper, and the Wedding Supper of the Lamb—which we'll discuss in depth in the final chapter. A kind of covenant meal was also a regular part of the Levitical offering system, where God, the priest, and the one bringing the offering would all get to enjoy a portion of the sacrifice together.

In Exodus 24:8, after Moses shared with Israel all the laws that God had given him and read to them from the Book of the Covenant, he ratified the covenant by sprinkling the people with blood: "Behold the blood of the covenant that the Lord has made with you in accordance with all these words." Afterward, Moses, Aaron and his two sons, and 70 of the elders ascended the mountain of the Lord and something magnificent happened. There on the mountain, these mere mortals, as the Scripture says, "saw the God of Israel." The only description they give is of the pavement under his feet, "of sapphire stone, like the very heaven for clearness." And there, in his presence, beholding God, they eat and they drink. These three verses paint a sublime picture of communion with God over a covenant meal, where the representatives of his people are swept up—yet unharmed—in the grandeur and majesty of their God. Covenant meals were a time for each party to reconfirm their commitment to its promises and to each other.

When Jesus associates his blood with the covenant, he is evoking this kind of meal. Connecting his blood with the new covenant specifically links all who drink of it to a specific series of promises reiterated throughout the Old Testament to reverse the ruin of exile after Israel's return to their land.

A unique feature of the new covenant was its emphasis on the heart. The Law would go from being written on tablets of stone to being written on the heart, where God would put his Spirit. Following the Law would shift inward from the external and ceremonial aspects of Law-keeping to the more spiritual, to what we are in our thoughts, attitudes, desires, and hidden places of our heart. Deuteronomy 30:6 says, "the LORD your God will circumcise your heart and the heart of your offspring, so that you will love the LORD your God with all your heart and with all your soul, that you may live." Mere observance of the Law had not won God their hearts. He didn't just want to be obeyed, but loved. Jeremiah 31:33 puts it this way: "This is the covenant that I will make with the house of Israel after those days, declares the LORD: I will put my law within them, and I will write it on their hearts. And I will be their God, and they shall be my people." The Law will live within them, on new tablets of flesh, not stone. To this point, Ezekiel 36:26 provides a near echo, "And I will give you a new heart, and a new spirit I will put within you. And I will remove the heart of stone from your flesh and give you a heart of flesh." The cup of which we drink is not just about obedience or forgiveness, but about our hearts.

What they'd hoped would happen after the remnant returned to Israel would come more fully with the advent of Christ, and it would come through the work of the Holy Spirit. The Lord's table, though instituted before Pentecost, looks forward to the giving of the Holy Spirit. And as we, on the other side of Pentecost, take part in it, we celebrate what new depth of fellowship we have with God through his Spirit residing within us, regenerating and renewing us, moving the slider that reverses ruin within our hearts. There could be no hope for true and complete renewal without the Spirit. By his emphasis on the heart, God makes it clear that he does not want detached obedience, but obedience borne of love. He wants our devotion and our affection. Thanks to Christ's blood, rather than having hard hearts, we can have tender and responsive ones. We have hearts that know God, love God, and respond to his work within us. Thus the cup speaks.

And the Holy Spirit does even more. Ezekiel 11:19 adds, "I will give them one heart." God will unify his people through his Spirit. By him, we are "being built together into a dwelling place for God" (Ephesians 2:22). The new covenant does not just renew and regenerate individuals but communities. Charles Ellicott notes, "Unity of purpose among the restored exiles was to be at once a consequence and a condition of their improved moral condition."[2] The new covenant didn't just open the way for malleable and loving hearts to seek renewal at the deepest levels, but to connect renewed hearts through the Spirit to one another. Since we all share the same Spirit, unity—yielding to one another, submitting to one another, honoring each other, trusting that you could afford to give more away in all aspects of life because you won't go hungry—testified to the Spirit's power, strength, and truth. So the blood not only regenerates individuals but the people of God corporately.

At my church, we take turns serving the bread and wine during the communion service. As congregants walk by, we say, "This is Christ's body, given for you," or "This is Christ's blood, poured out for you." There have been times I have been shaken from feelings of alienation from someone with whom I bitterly disagree when I've had to look them in the eye and say, "This is Christ's body, given for you." The gravity of the exchange and the value of that person to Christ is so impressed upon me that any animosity I feel for them, in that moment, melts away. These disagreements are not disagreements with enemies, but with brothers and sisters purchased by the same blood and adopted into the same family fellowshipping with the same Christ through the same Spirit. I cannot at the same time serve them the bread or wine and harbor ill will toward them. For me, the first step in resolving conflict with them happens at the table, seeing their same need for the same graces that I myself have received and would be utterly lost without. I know they're journeying along the same sanctification process by the Spirit that I am. We're taking the same road and getting lost and needing so much grace to get there. Recognizing that they are as much in need of the table as I am, that they are as welcomed and forgiven as I am, reminds me that, just like the older brother, as the younger comes to the table repentant, our relationship can be healed.

A Table for One

We are hardwired to connect more closely with those with whom we eat similar foods. Researchers have found that eating similar foods stimulates feelings of trust and cooperation between people who are otherwise strangers. Communion was a meal to be shared, both with God and among his people. The importance of unity among God's people cannot be overstated. The early church did not have church buildings as we do today, so they met in homes (Acts 2:46; Romans 16:5; 1 Corinthians 16:19; Philemon 2). The Lord's supper was a meal taken around the table at someone's house. It was and is a family meal. It is a grace bestowed on the collective, renewing not just our relationship with God but with each other. The table does something to us together.

Paul talks about the practice of the Lord's supper at a house church in 1 Corinthians. He receives a report that the church there was gathering in an every-man-for-themselves manner, where "one man goes hungry, another man gets drunk." Paul rebukes them for it; this couldn't be farther from the spirit of fellowship that pervades the meals God ordains or his desire for his people. New Testament scholar Richard Hays notes, "Paul's vision of community comes into conflict with the Corinthians' conventional social mores, which require distinctions of rank and status to be recognized at table: the more privileged members expect to receive more and better food than others."[3] Jesus had taught against this very dynamic at banquets. God had embedded community safety nets in feasts as well. At Passover, you invited individuals and smaller families to join you to reduce their burden. For the Feast of Weeks, you left the edges of your field for the vulnerable and those who were poor and landless. For Sukkot, you invited the marginalized into your *sukkah*. When the remnant went through revival, you prepared portions for those who had none. But now, at the Lord's table, a recognition of the greatest deliverance yet—bigger than exodus, bigger than settling in Canaan, bigger than returning after exile—they thought only of themselves. This was never to be the spirit of the Lord's meals, where those of lesser means were always to be taken care of. Theologian Ronald Hesselgrave writes, "Paul is clear that the treatment of the poor believers is inconsistent with and, in fact, contradicts the fellowship and union with Christ which is expressed in the Lord's Supper."[4] To call it the Lord's supper was to take his name in vain, to use his name to represent something it was never meant to represent, and, in fact, quite antithetical to his character. Richard Hays writes, "Paul declares that—contrary to what they may suppose—what they are eating is not in fact 'the Lord's Supper'; it is their own private meal."[5] When Jesus gave his initial instructions for the meal, one of the very first things he said before explaining what the elements meant was, "Take this, and divide it among yourselves" (Luke 22:17). He told them to share. They could claim no true understanding of the table, no transformational fellowship with Christ, no appetite for his kingdom, if they were selfish at his very table. Hesselgrave continues, "By using the Lord's Supper as the occasion for reaffirming social privilege, hierarchy and division within the Christian community, Paul says, the 'haves' are expressing utter contempt for the church and humiliating the 'have nots' within the community."[6] They have eaten the bread and drunk the cup in a manner unworthy of the Lord. Paul's teaching moment on the essence of the Lord's Supper came not as a response to private shortcomings, but to interpersonal ones.

PROCLAIM THE LORD'S DEATH

Communion is also a sign for the world. While those outside the body of Christ do not share the meal, they can feel and observe the effects of it through what we do. They benefit from the individual and corporate formation that accompanies our meal. Our return to humility, generosity, mercy, and peacemaking after partaking in this meal mindfully and in earnest finds full expression on the edges of our fields, on our battlefields, and at our own tables as well. Here, and in all the many other places touched by the fruit of communion, we meet our unbelieving neighbor. Here they learn if this meal we take is sheer pageantry or power.

Just as Israel's memory of Egypt was the basis for obedience to some commands, the same can be true for us in how the tastes of the table linger between meals. This is what it means when Paul says we proclaim Christ's death (1 Corinthians 11:26): we do not just let the message of it come from our lips, but the beauty and efficacy of it radiate from our lives. When the table lingers between meals no one loves their enemy better than we do: we are quickest to serve others, we are longsuffering, we do not live in fear of losing ground to our neighbor, instead we truly put others' interests above our own. "Those who fail to embody this love within their own lives make a mockery of Jesus' death."[7]

REMEMBRANCE AND PARTICIPATION

We live starved for our story. Communion helps us. We pause to remember the deep things, the mysteries, the challenges, and the beauty.

Our stories are nested in Christ's and, as we share in the bread and cup, we revisit and reclaim its power. We don't only want to remember, but we do need to remember. In this, the Spirit helps. Research Professor J. Todd Billings writes, "The Spirit shows, offers, and communicates Jesus Christ to believers at the Supper."[8] We learn him in new and deeper ways, digesting him more fully than the time before, smelling of him as we go from the table, sharing with others about the best meal we had. But Communion isn't all cerebral either. "The Lord's Supper is more than a mental act of meaning making. It is an embodied practice in community, engaging all our senses in the context of worship."[9]

His Benefits to Us

We know we are united with Christ. But what are the advantages of this union? When we feed on his flesh and drink his blood, we abide in him and he in us. He justified, purified, and redeemed us with the sprinkling of his matchless blood. In Christ, God delivered us from the present evil age and from fear of death and delivered us into the kingdom of his beloved Son, where fear does not exist. Christ disarmed the rulers and authorities of this age, putting them to open shame. Through him we have overcome this world, being crucified to it, and it to us. We are made alive with him by his Spirit, that he might bring us to God; possessing him, possessing life itself. Long before time began, he foreordained us as a family for his glory. In him, we have the forgiveness of sins both known and hidden. Our inheritance—glorious, rich, imperishable, unfading—comes from him. He calls us to a better hope.

Until the Kingdom of God Comes

Communion is also a bridge from the past to the future wedding feast we await. It has one foot in Christ's first coming and one foot in his second, and its body hovers over the middle. N.T. Wright writes,

All of this is summed up in a brilliant little sentence in 1 Corinthians 11.26. "Whenever you eat this bread and drink this cup," says Paul, "you announce the Lord's death until he comes." The present moment ("whenever") somehow holds together the one-off past event ("the Lord's death") and the great future when God's world will be remade under Jesus' loving rule ("until he comes"). Past and future come rushing together into the present, pouring an ocean of meaning into the little bottle of "now."[10]

Communion is both reflection and foretaste. It remembers and awaits. It overwinters while it anticipates a future fullness. It pitches a *sukkah* and remembers God sustains. It reminds us we live in that gloriously unsettled middle while fixing our eyes on an even more glorious end. Billings writes, "The Lord's Supper, as a foretaste of the wedding banquet of the Lamb and his bride, gives us a taste of God's new world."[11] Taken correctly, it is a preview of the banquet to come.

COMING TO THE TABLE

I have asked myself, while holding the bread and cup, can I, with these few seconds, properly prepare for what's about to take place? And the answer is no. The time to prepare for the table is during life itself: during trials and temptations, in the unhurried rhythms of everyday, and in our pursuit of things like beauty, glory, and belonging. It's in our lived union with Christ, not a theoretical one, where we find the most to chew on at his table. Not just in the 45 seconds of reflection that precede it.

LITURGY FOR THE LORD'S SUPPER

INVITATION

Come, brothers and sisters, come join your family for this sacred meal.

Come penitent, come captive, come hungry, and be fed.

A feast has been spread sufficient for your needs, pleasing to your palate, and filling for your soul.

Let none go hungry; come eat its blessed fare.

CONFESSION

Lord, we confess we have put other things before you. We have led unreconciled lives with each other and with you. We have obscured your image by our division, we have left others behind while we rush ahead, and we have lived unexamined lives indistinguishable from the world. We have glanced longingly after Egypt, kept the edges of our fields for ourselves, and trusted our city walls. Have mercy on us, O God. Grant us undivided hearts that we may, with hearts of flesh on which your law is now written, truly love you and our neighbor before a watching world. And may our whole heart, soul, mind, strength, and very being, seek its nutriment in you.

Pardon

Angels rejoice over you, forgiven one, for turning to Christ from sin. By his blood, you who were once far off have been brought near and have been reconciled to God in one body through the cross. By his blood, you have been spared from the death to come. You have peace with the God who welcomes strays home, not counting their sin against them or treating them as they deserve, but lavishing them with gifts of honor. This table is spread for you. Receive his freeing and cheering pardon.

Proclamation:

Once we were not a people but now we belong to you and each other

Thanks be to the body and blood of Christ

We have been ransomed and born again of imperishable seed

Thanks be to the body and blood of Christ

We have been adopted into a new family that is every one for each other

Thanks be to the body and blood of Christ

We have the same power working within us who raised Christ from the dead

Thanks be to the body and blood of Christ

We are recipients of a better covenant and better hope

Thanks be to the body and blood of Christ

He bore our sin that we might die to sin and live for him

Thanks be to the body and blood of Christ

Through him, we have eternal comfort, good hope, and courage

Thanks be to the body and blood of Christ

We have been re-created in the likeness of God and he will work in us his own glory

Thanks be to the body and blood of Christ

We have been privileged, in union with Christ, to suffer for his name's sake

Thanks be to the body and blood of Christ

He will present us without spot or blemish before his eternal throne

Thanks be to the body and blood of Christ

We can enter his rest and join in his joy

Thanks be to the body and blood of Christ

We can eat from a well-spread table that fills and secures

Thanks be to the body and blood of Christ

Chapter 12

MARRIAGE SUPPER OF THE LAMB

To the One Who Overcomes

I heard what seemed to be the voice of a great multitude, like the roar of many waters
and like the sound of mighty peals of thunder, crying out, "Hallelujah!
For the Lord our God the Almighty reigns.
Let us rejoice and exult and give him the glory, for the marriage of the Lamb has come,
and his Bride has made herself ready; it was granted her to clothe herself with fine linen,
bright and pure"—for the fine linen is the righteous deeds of the saints.

REVELATION 19:6-8

Beautiful, majestic, exalted, the mountain of the Lord stood. She was the joy of all creation. With citadels high and ramparts wide and all within her at peace, laughter and gladness rang forth through her bright, sunless sky. Behold! From her peaks descended the betrothed. The bride, exquisite, beamed like a star set in the midnight sky. She smelled of cedar and hyssop, of evergreen groves and the midwinter frost. Her devoted bridegroom, adorned in full regalia and decorated with a hole in each hand, eagerly joined her. He smelled warm and sweet—a mix of myrrh, aloe, and cassia. Though the panorama of paradise and myriad upon myriad of angels surrounded them, they held firm each other's gaze, just as they'd done while apart. Scrupulous preparation had been made for this very hour; the time was no longer nigh, but come.

With the wedding supper of the Lamb, we arrive at the feast to end all feasts. Like the final movement of a symphony where all leitmotifs, in turn, reappear in their most majestic form, every feast we've looked at leads to and resurges in this celebration. It is the culmination of the Old Testament's mandated festivals: our deliverance is complete and desert wandering over, the day of harvest has come, and the perfected are made holy. The feasts of the poets find their full expression here too: it is the Conqueror's final victory, the thirsty drink from the unending water of life, and Lady Wisdom's path reaches its end. Prophetic feasts are now fully realized: we are made better than new and all traces of ruin are reversed. The return from exile reaches a most satisfying conclusion: mourning is never to return. Sin is behind us and can reach no further.

The feasts of the Gospels are brought to fruition here as well: the repentant are welcomed home and cloaked in robes of grace they could never have earned. The last, at last, are first, and the humble, exalted. Jesus once more eats of the Passover meal, because its meaning is fulfilled in this kingdom; his union with his people is complete.

A Persecuted and World-Weary Church

Revelation was written as an exhortation to churches throughout Asia Minor suffering from persecution. As with all prophetic and apocalyptic literature, Revelation is future-oriented. But, as a letter, its future orientation is intended to encourage its contemporary audience, the first-century church, to patiently endure and to reassure them that their steadfastness was not in vain.

Amid intense trials, the persecuted church needed some key that could provide a sense of scale for their experience: to see that what felt long was really short, that what felt unbearable could be borne, that what seemed important was actually trivial, that what appeared to reign did not do so unchecked, and that what felt like losses were really gains. New Testament scholar Dennis Johnson writes, "On the plane of visible history things are not what they appear, so Revelation's symbols make things appear as they are."[1] In a word, what the church needed was perspective.

Revelation gave them much-needed vision that countered what their naked eye saw. Where they saw defeat, Revelation showed them that in the end, only two would conquer: Christ and those who follow him to the end. Anything contrary to these would pass away. The defeat they felt and experienced would not be final.

Not only would they conquer, but they and the Lamb would conquer in the same way: not through power, religious nationalism, or political maneuvering to establish an earthly kingdom, but in humbly committing themselves to Word and witness, and sacrificing now for the kingdom to come, where their true citizenship lay. The Ellicott commentary states that those who conquer are those who, "like their Master, refused to win power by doing homage to wrong...Wherever the Church has illegitimately grasped at power, she has lost it."[2] They could wield no power so great as their witness for Christ.

Beyond correcting their vision, Revelation also showed these early Christians that their suffering in the name of Christ and his kingdom contributed to a cosmic cause; their commitment and witness were not in vain but were indispensable to the epic of redemption. Their works would not be swallowed up by this world, but rather, as Revelation 14:13 says, "Their deeds follow them!" Their Christ-exalting deeds made up the fiber of that white linen wedding garment Christ's bride would one day wear.

Revelation affirmed that their hardships were short and preparatory, their steadfastness was their victory, and their present toiling contributed to a greater future purpose. The same is true for us and gives
us hope. Johnson writes,

> Revelation's last word is not about the destructive power
> of the "prince of darkness grim" but rather about the
> joyful celebration of those redeemed by Jesus, the Lord's
> Messiah. This hope motivates the suffering church to
> endure tribulation and the tempted church to remain a
> pure bride for her Groom.[3]

The joy God promised on the far side of endurance was sure.

Years ago, on a trip to Indonesia, I was eager to see a performance of
wayang kulit, Javanese shadow puppetry. A typical performance could
last from dusk until dawn. One evening after sundown, I arrived at an
open square with a translucent screen on short risers set up in its center.
The puppeteers sat on one side with their ornate and intricately crafted
puppets, or *wayang*, representing characters in Hindu epics, and the
gamelan orchestra. On the other side sat the audience. The way they
set the stage, however, you could watch from either side. If you just
wanted to see the shadow of the puppets, you would sit on the dark
side of the screen. But if you, like I, were mesmerized with the puppets
themselves, the movements of the puppeteers, and the synchronized
strikes of the gamelan, you could sit on the lit side that controlled and
created the shadows. We spend our lives on the shadow side, where
distortion and mystery abound, but we forget it is ultimately light that
controls the shadows. Revelation shows us that.

Flush with imagery of darkness and evil—beast, dragon, prostitute,
Death and Hades, false prophets, and the deceiver himself—Revelation portrays the reign of terror as interim and destined for demise. We
are quick to console ourselves and each other when life gets tough with,

"It's temporary." Like us, the early church needed finish lines, even if they were but one leg of a long relay. They could use the reminder that evil may be having a moment, but that a moment was all it had. Darkness would expire. And in its place, bliss, as of a bridegroom taking his bride, would resound throughout eternity. There would be no dirge for the passing of darkness, only a wedding hymn for Christ and his readied bride.

SEEING THEMSELVES IN THE BOOK

"Representation matters" is a popular saying among minorities today. To see ourselves in others who have "made it" in some arena expands our imagination for our future and motivates us to persevere. We aspire to higher heights and are inspired to stay the course despite opposition. Seeing someone like us end up somewhere so drastically beyond their beginnings is extremely powerful. We also know, deep in the marrow of our tiniest bone, that the promise of eventual judgment against workers of injustice can sustain an otherwise backbreaking call. It can lift us from a sense of futile purposelessness, so we no longer think ourselves laboring in vain.

Early Christians were religious minorities, and they could see themselves and their trials in the backstory of the bride. They were not suffering from revoked privileges, for their sole privilege as Christians was bearing the name of Christ and being granted to suffer for him. They faced prison and death (Revelation 2:10, 13). In one of John's visions, he saw the souls of those who had been slain for the word of God and the witness they'd borne, crying out, "How long before you will judge?" (Revelation 6:10), a question they themselves had almost certainly asked before. But in another vision, just before the wedding takes place, John sees a multitude singing of the avenged blood of the slain (Revelation 19:2). The Bride consisted of those who had overcome the tribulations and not been seduced by the evil one. She, held firm by God, in turn held firm to his Word and bore witness to him. The avenged were among her ranks.

It wasn't just the bride's backstory the church saw themselves in. Scorned, mocked, and facing death, they also saw their story in the Lamb who was slain. There was a beautiful resonance in their stories. What a comfort to know the Lamb could fully understand where his bride was coming from and what she was going through, the pressures and snares and fickleness of the world. He had suffered for her and, though it both broke and stirred his heart, she was suffering because of her love for him now too.

The Occasion

There's an Indian parable about blind men and an elephant. Several blind men touch different parts of an elephant and describe what they feel. Each description varies widely from the next. Completely unfamiliar with elephants, their already limited descriptions are further constrained by being reliant on the language of what they know.

So it is with the wedding feast. In Revelation, when John describes the eventual union of Christ and the church, he describes it multiple times, each time placing his hands on a different part of it. Even after he's run his hands over all that he—a finite creature—can, the union, just like the elephant, is far more than the composite of his descriptions.

Though John blesses the guests in Revelation 19:9—"Blessed are those who are invited to the marriage supper of the Lamb"—we find images of the wedding throughout. We will look at their composite. We must start our exploration, however, with Jewish wedding customs.

Jewish Weddings

Jewish weddings are two-stage affairs. The first stage is the betrothal. In modern American English usage, this word is fairly archaic and considered interchangeable with engagement. But the original audience would have envisioned something more binding. Betrothal was the beginning of a contractual relationship between a couple. In the eyes of the Law, from betrothal forward, the couple was formally married. That is why Joseph, though only betrothed to Mary, would have had to divorce her if he no longer wished to marry her. Marriage effectively preceded the wedding.

During the betrothal, however, the couple lived separately from each other, each with their own family. It was a time of preparation for the bride and, for each, a time of waiting. The bride waited for some future appointed date when her husband would take her from her parents' house to his own. The groom would prepare a place for her on his father's land. The bride would prepare her wedding garments and keep herself pure.

With the betrothal also came the paying of the dowry, or the bride price. Whether in goods or in service, a price had to be paid.[4] Once everything was ready, the wedding feast would take place.

The wedding supper of the Lamb will be the climax of this two-stage marriage process. Christ's incarnation was the betrothal, his taking on flesh. His life was the bride price, his shed blood ransoming people from every tribe, language, people, and nation (Revelation 5:9). The period between Christ's first and second coming is the time of preparation. What feels like forever for the bride flashes by in a moment for the Lamb. And then one day, sweet mercy of mercies, the bride will become bone of his bone and flesh of his flesh as Eden erupts in breathless praise and the gospel reaches full flower.

The image of a future wedding feast told the church then, and the church now, all they needed to know about the present—it was relatively short, it was a time of preparation, and Christ was covenantally bound to them. It also told them about their future—that one day they would at last come together face-to-face with their Love, becoming one flesh, mesmerized and electrified by each other's beauty and perfection, and reveling in an enviable intimacy that rocked time and creation. This was the blessed consummation of their trajectories. Above all, it taught them to see their trials and tribulations—and history itself—through the lens of God as a tireless wedding planner.

Throughout the process, we see God everywhere and in all things at work. The Father chooses the bride and sends his Son to pay the bride price. After the Son returns to his Father's side, he sends his Spirit to his bride to preserve her during her time of preparation, and himself intercedes with the Father on her behalf. Father, Son, and Spirit all, at various times and in different ways, invite to the feast.

THE BRIDEGROOM

Throughout Revelation, the bridegroom appears in many guises. He's the son of man, dressed in a long robe dipped in blood, with a golden sash across his chest, a sharp two-edged sword in his sheath, a golden diadem on his head, a sickle in his hand, and a face shining like the sun in full strength. The new heavens and new earth have no sun because he himself is their light. He's the holder of the seven stars, the Alpha and Omega, the first and the last. He's the Son of God, with eyes like flames of fire, feet like burnished bronze, and the voice of a trumpet. He's the holy and true one, holder of the key of David, who opens and no one shuts, who shuts and no one opens. He's the Amen, the faithful and true witness, the beginning of God's creation. He's the Lion of the tribe of Judah, the Root of David, who alone can open the scroll revealing what must come to pass. He's the male child caught up to God who will rule the nations. He is Lord of lords and King of kings—names tattooed on his thigh and written on his robe—and he's conqueror of the beast. He's the rider on the white horse, he's called Faithful and True, Word of God. He's the sole temple and sun of New Jerusalem and the bright morning star. But the name on his wedding announcement is Lamb.

John, more than any other New Testament writer, employs the imagery of a lamb. He uses *Lamb* as the main title for Jesus in Revelation a total of 28 times, and it is found throughout his Gospel as well. Lamb imagery originates in the Old Testament. In Genesis 22, when Abraham climbs Mount Moriah at God's command with Isaac, his promised only son, God himself provides the lamb for the offering. Next, we see the lamb in the Passover, its blood smeared on the doorposts sparing the people, a significant turning point in the redemption of God's people.

In the New Testament, the Lamb appears in John's Gospel. John the Baptist sees Jesus approaching him and declares, "Behold, the Lamb of God, who takes away the sins of the world!" (John 1:29). In 1 Corinthians 5, as we saw earlier in the Passover chapter, Paul describes Jesus as our Passover lamb. Peter connects the church with the lamb in 1 Peter 1:19, saying we were ransomed from our futile ways with the precious blood of Christ, "like that of a lamb without blemish or spot." Spurgeon wrote, "How fine a picture of Christ. No other creature could so well have typified him who was holy, harmless, undefiled, and separate from sinners...so gentle and innocent, so mild and harmless, neither hurting others, nor seeming to have the power to resent an injury."[5] Elsewhere, and for her benefit, Christ is fierce, regal, divine, and cosmic sovereign, but when it comes to his lasting union with his bride, he is sacrificial, tender, lowly.

THE BRIDE

The bride, the church, was a sight to behold—unified, diverse, perfected. She'd been cleansed in the water of the word and had made herself ready during the betrothal. Her white linen robe, bright and pure, had been washed in the blood of the Lamb and spun from the righteous deeds of the saints. It was an heirloom and the finest of God's handiwork, and he'd given it to her to put on. Like the Lamb, she had neither spot nor blemish. In her hands, she held palm branches, an emblem of triumph. Topping her head, the crown of life. With tearless eyes and lifted head, in splendor, she stood erect. The Lamb himself had given her his glory, and she had captivated his heart. She was the holy city, the new Jerusalem, the assembly of the firstborn.

In her glory, the bride is a mixed multitude from all nations, tribes, tongues, and peoples. Revelation 7:9 says, "Behold, a great multitude that no one could number, from every nation, from all tribes and peoples and languages, standing before the throne and before the Lamb." But the seeds of a multiethnic bride were planted as far back as Genesis, in the Abrahamic covenant when God said to Abram, "No longer shall your name be called Abram, but your name shall be Abraham, for I have made you the father of *a multitude of nations*" (Genesis 17:5, emphasis mine). Later in Genesis 18:18, the Lord reaffirms this plan, "Abraham shall surely become a great and mighty nation, and all the nations of the earth shall be blessed in him."

In Luke and Acts, the Gentile expansion of God's kingdom is emphasized in the parable of the Good Samaritan (Luke 10:35-37), Jesus' parting words—"You will be my witnesses in Jerusalem and in all Judea and Samaria, and to the end of the earth,"—at the ascension (Acts 1:8), and, most notably, at Pentecost (Acts 2:1-13). The Great Commission also reveals Christ's intent for his gospel to reach the farthest ends of the earth through the ministry of his disciples, "Go therefore and make disciples of all nations" (Matthew 28:19).

These all show us God's multinational and multiethnic vision for his church. Its diversity is not a new enterprise, afterthought, or product of an increasingly globalized world. But, rather, God intended it from the establishing of his people. The bride's beauty is inseparable from her diversity. Her multiculturalism is neither incidental nor accidental. It is worldwide and all-encompassing because that bears witness to the preeminence of God and his gospel as well as the supremacy of faith over ethnic background in salvation. Just as there is no place within a person God cannot reach, there is no place among people he cannot reach. He penetrates deep and wide. The chorus the multitude will sing before the throne will be sung in countless languages; even those languages now dead will be revived at his throne to praise the Lamb. As Hendriksen wrote, "there is nothing narrow or national about this redemption."[6]

What makes the bride's diversity even more spectacular is its unity. You might expect to have one or the other, and it's quite easy to look at the world and see why that may be so. But God has something better planned for his people, something supernatural and set apart from the world.

Where God penetrates, he works to make whole. The bride is undivided: in affections, whole-hearted; in constitution, united; within her, there are no divisions. When Jesus prayed his high priestly prayer, he prayed for the church he would soon leave behind. He asked, "Holy Father, keep them in your name, which you have given me, *that they may be one*, even as we are one" (John 17:11, emphasis mine). Jesus asks for this twice in his prayer, and each time the church's unity flows from the oneness of God, "even as we are one." Unity was to be a defining feature of his church because it was a defining feature of her God. We seek unity as the bride because our beloved is one and we aspire to reflect his character and beauty.

But there was another reason the church was to be one. In John 17:23, Jesus says it is "so that the world may know that you sent me and love them even as you loved me." Our unity is a witness to the world and the result of God's love perfected within us. The world will look to our oneness as proof of God's love. True unity, then, must be something the internalized love of God could produce. The love of God erases lines of division between Greek and Jew, circumcised and uncircumcised, barbarian and Scythian, slave and free, male and female.

Romans 12:5 says, "We, though many, are one body in Christ, and individually members one of another." The love of God broke down the dividing wall of hostility between Jew and Gentile and between sinner and God. Unity was her privilege, her joy, and her call.

THE VENUE

The Lamb and bride wed in paradise. Christ, the second Adam. The bride, the second Eve. They were surrounded by innumerable angels in festal gathering. The smoke of the incense, with the prayers of the saints, rose before the throne. The multitude sang a new song, the song of the redeemed.

When we arrive at the wedding feast, realities now encased in inadequate words will become gloriously concrete. Everything now hinted and shadowed will be made sublimely manifest. Our souls and senses will be inundated with the realization of the ignorance of what we now call knowledge and of the shallowness of what we now call depth. We will see the great chasm that yawns between our highest thoughts and the most basic of divine realities. Ours will join a sea of busied hands— some raised in praise, some clapping in jubilant wonder, some wiping tears of joy from the corner of their awe-filled eyes. A whole new language for worship will ring forth, but more importantly, the force of a whole new understanding will propel its chorus forward from our lips. And though many-tongued the throng, they will sing in unison, "Hallelujah," Hebrew for "Praise Yahweh."

And a bliss that no one has known will inflame our souls. The song of the merry hearted will reverberate across creation. We will sing with abandon, each in our own tongue, of the God of wonder and might. Lighthearted, we will dance till we've worn out the ground, and our feet cry mercy. Gladness will spread its canopy from east to west. The sound of instruments will mix with great peals of uncontainable laughter. The voice of the bride and bridegroom will once and forevermore be heard.

The only inequality felt there will be the love between Lamb and bride. We will always, throughout eternity, be more loved than we love. Even perfected and glorified, our love will not contend with his, but be enveloped and warmed and instigated by it. We will reach the end of insufficiency. At all times and in every way, we have all we need. The weariness in our souls from comparing who we are and what we have with others will cease. There will be no deception. We will know the truth about ourselves and see ourselves the way God always wanted us to see. Then we will know in full, and by knowing obtain eternal life.

Not only will death and danger be defeated, but hope and faith will become obsolete. As Paul said, who hopes for what we already have (Romans 8:24)? Or the author of Hebrews, "Hope that is seen is no hope at all" (Hebrews 11:1). We will possess all we've spent our days hoping for. Paul says in 1 Corinthians 13:13, "So now faith, hope, and love abide, these three; but the greatest of these is love." That is because love outlasts the others. It will exist into eternity, but faith and hope will fall away like boosters on a space rocket that launch it beyond earth's orbit. We need them for the journey, but not the destination.

CHRIST CALLS "COME"

So many of our questions come down to this: Will I make it? Will this all work out? Into your captivity, waiting, wilderness, sin, battles, shame, small beginnings, marginalization, backsliding, competition, poverty, disability, fatigue, and persecution Christ calls, "Come."

Our Deliverer says, "Come."

Our Sustainer says, "Come."

Our Perfector says, "Come."

Our Warrior says, "Come."

Our Thirst Quencher says, "Come."

Our Wisdom says, "Come."

Our Hope says, "Come."

Our Strength says, "Come."

Our Exalter says, "Come."

Our Father says, "Come."

Our Food and Drink says, "Come."

Come know the fullness of the Bridegroom's table. Come, taste and see that he is good. Though we come to him empty-handed, we find him ever and always abounding in steadfast love and faithfulness. His table is a smorgasbord of grace where we, the beloved, make ourselves at home.

Amid intense trials, God reassured his church he would triumph over evil and that his Son would take his bride. The betrothal period, however dark it may get, would culminate in a rapturous fulfillment of that promise God made in Exodus 6:7 when he assured Moses he'd deliver his people, "I will take you to be my people, and I will be your God." Revelation 21:3 says, "And I heard a loud voice from the throne saying, 'Behold, the dwelling place of God is with man. He will dwell with them, and they will be his people and God himself will be with them as their God.'" We will enter the incandescent joy of our Lord, our Maker, our Love.

The Invited Become the Inviters

God does not just allay our fears about survival, but his table turns us into channels of the grace we ourselves have savored. Once we have tasted of his table, we give others a taste. We help lead others—both body and soul—out of captivity. We allow ourselves to be used by God as tools in each other's growth, helping to water each other's faith, encouraging each other daily, speaking to one another in psalms and hymns and spiritual songs, pointing one another back to Scripture and to living not by the flesh but by the Spirit.

We confess our sins to one other that we may be healed and remind each other of the times in our wildernesses where God has sustained us and even now sustains. We live lives of cruciform victory and celebrate true triumph, not making this path seem easy, but possible with God and worth it for the joy before us. When we cling to God in our deserts, it gives others the courage to hold onto him in theirs too; when we finally leave those deserts, we pack up its fruit to share with others back home like souvenirs. We invite others into wisdom by sharing what we know, being open to rebuke, and lovingly rebuking others.

When we live as people of hope, despite all we can see, looking forward to eventual renewal, we draw others into seeing what we see. When our city walls are our God and are repaired by understanding, others look into rebuilding theirs too. By unshackling ourselves from even the subtlest ways status rules our lives—ending the chase and making our tables wide—we invite others to do so as well. When we are secure in our acceptance by God, rather than slaving away after it, and can lay to rest all other such strivings, it invites others to do the same.

When mercied people mercy people, others want to taste what they're having too. Hospitality is great, but the overflow of a life fully satisfied at God's table is more powerful than our best-dressed table. By frequenting his table and partaking of all it has to offer, we become inviting people who invite people because we've been invited. We, too, say, "Come."

LITURGY FOR UNITY

The One my soul loves,
make me beautiful for you
no matter the cost.
If tears are for my beauty, I will shed them.
If loss is for my beauty, I will part in peace.
If suffering is for my beauty, I will endure.
If scars are for my beauty, I will take courage.
If persecution is for my beauty, I will cleave.
If mocking is for my beauty, I will listen to a sweeter song.
If obscurity is for my beauty, I will steward it well.
If being last place is for my beauty, I will mount my prize.
If hunger and thirst are for my beauty, I will eat from a higher
table.
Whatever may be for my beauty, do not hesitate to send.
And may my life thrill you to watch
as I transform my beauty into yours
that our beauty may be alike.

Benediction

Now may the God who feasts our
weary souls with gladness

and unites us together through his
Spirit as we eat of one loaf,

restore and keep us

at all times and in every way

by the blood of the eternal covenant,

and bring us safely into his radiant presence,

having withstood the weight of the
worry that seeks to break us.

To him be glory, majesty, dominion, and authority

both now and to the day of eternity.

To those loved at a wide table,

he who calls you is faithful;

he will do it.

Grace be with you all.

Notes

CHAPTER 1

1. Hebrew for *commandment.*
2. Hebrew for *Passover.*
3. *Mishnah Pesachim* 10:1.
4. James K. Bruckner, *Exodus: Understanding the Bible Commentary Series* (Ada, MI: Baker Publishing Group, 2012), 88.
5. J.A. Motyer, *The Message of Exodus: The Days of Our Pilgrimage* (Downers Grove, IL: InterVarsity Press, 2005), 115.
6. Motyer, *The Message of Exodus,* 161.
7. The rabbinic period circa 1st–6th centuries.
8. John S. Allen, *The Omnivorous Mind: Our Evolving Relationship with Food* (Cambridge, MA: Harvard University Press, 2012), 151-152,158.
9. *Pesachim* 116b.
10. Alasdair MacIntyre, *After Virtue* (United Kingdom: Bloomsbury Publishing, 2013), 250.
11. James K. Bruckner, *Exodus Commentary* (Peabody, MA: Hendrickson Publishers, 2008), 170.
12. D. Brown, A.R. Fausset, and R. Jamieson, *A Commentary, Critical, Experimental, and Practical, on the Old and New Testaments: Genesis–Deuteronomy, vol. I* (London; Glasgow: William Collins, Sons, & Company, Limited, n.d.), 309.
13. Richard Booker, *Celebrating Jesus in the Biblical Feasts* (Shippensburg, PA: Destiny Image Publishers, 2016), 67.
14. Philip Ryken, *Exodus: Saved for God's Glory* (Wheaton, IL: Crossway, 2005), 503.

CHAPTER 2

1. M.F. Rooker, *Leviticus vol. 3A* (Nashville, TN: Broadman & Holman Publishers, 2000), 281.
2. David Weston Baker, Dale A. Brueggemann, Philip Wesley Comfort, Eugene H. Merril, *Leviticus, Numbers, Deuteronomy, vol. 2* (Carol Stream, IL: Tyndale House Publishers, 1996), 167.
3. Rooker, *Leviticus, vol. 3A,* 282.

4. Ibid., 286.

5. "Firstfruits and Pentecost," Ligonier Ministries, accessed April 22, 2021, www.ligonier.org/learn/devotionals/firstfruits-and-pentecost/.

6. An identical command appears in Leviticus 19:9-10, headlining instructions on how to love your neighbor and again in Deuteronomy 24:19-22 with the promise that God would bless their obedience. The threefold repetition underscored its importance.

7. Jerram Barrs, *Delighting in the Law of the Lord: God's Alternative to Legalism and Moralism* (Wheaton, IL: Crossway, 2013), 105,104.

8. Ronald H. Isaacs, *Every Person's Guide to Shavuot* (Lanham, MD: Jason Aronson, 1999), 5.

9. Iain M. Duguid, *Numbers: God's Presence in the Wilderness* (Wheaton, IL: Crossway, 2012), 315.

10. Jeremiah 31:31-34; Ezekiel 36:22-28; and Deuteronomy 30:6.

11. Mikeal C. Parsons, *Acts in Paideia: Commentaries on the New Testament* (Grand Rapids: Baker Academic, 2008), 36.

12. I. Howard Marshall, *Acts: An Introduction and Commentary* (Nottingham, UK: InterVarsity Press/IVP Academic, 2008), 94.

13. Clement of Alexandria, Stromata 7.7.

CHAPTER 3

1. Gordon J. Wenham, *The Book of Leviticus* (Grand Rapids, MI: Eerdmans Publishing Company, 1994), 5.

2. Richard Booker, *Celebrating Jesus in the Biblical Feasts* (Shippensburg, PA: Destiny Image Publishers, 2016), 113.

3. George Bradford Caird, "The Exegetical Method of the Epistle to the Hebrews," *Canadian Journal of Theology* 5 (1959), 47.

4. Irving Greenberg, *The Jewish Way: Living the Jewish Holidays* (New York: Touchstone, 2011), 141.

5. Frederick Buechner, *A Room Called Remember* (San Francisco, CA: HarperOne, 2009), 61.

6. Greenberg, *The Jewish Way*, 149.

7. Ibid., 145.

8. Based on the Shehecheyanu blessing ("Who has given us life"), a common Jewish prayer said to celebrate special occasions, especially firsts or unusual circumstances.

CHAPTER 4

1. Mark D. Futato, The Book of Psalms, in *Cornerstone Biblical Commentary, vol. 7: The Book of Psalms, The Book of Proverbs* (Carol Stream, IL: Tyndale House Publishers, 2009), 102.

2. John Goldingay, *Psalms: Volume 1: Psalms 1–41* (Ada, MI: Baker Publishing Group, 2006), 349.

3. Ibid., 350.

4. Frederick Buechner, *Secrets in the Dark* (San Francisco, CA: HarperOne, 2009), 128.

5. Goldingay, *Psalms: Volume 1,* 354.

6. Spurgeon Commentary, https://www.studylight.org/commentaries/eng/spe /psalms-23.html.

7. Derek Kidner, *Psalms 1–72* (Downers Grove: InterVarsity Press, 2014), 129.

8. Ibid.

9. Nancy L. deClaisse-Walford, Rolf A. Jacobson, and Beth LaNeel Tanner, *The Book of Psalms,* The New International Commentary on the Old Testament (Grand Rapids, MI: Eerdmans Publishing Company, 2014), 241.

10. B. K. Waltke, J. M. Houston, & E. Moore, *The Psalms as Christian Worship: A Historical Commentary* (Grand Rapids, MI; Cambridge, U.K.: William B. Eerdmans Publishing Company, 2010), 442-43.

11. Gerald H. Wilson, *Psalms Volume 1* (Grand Rapids, MI: Zondervan, 2014), 631.

12. Ibid., 641.

CHAPTER 5

1. Derek Kidner, *Psalms 1–72* (Downers Grove: InterVarsity Press, 2014), 242.

2. Psalm 63:1.

3. John Goldingay, *Psalms: Volume 2 Psalms 42–89* (Ada, MI: Baker Publishing Group, 2007), 257.

4. Craig C. Broyles, *Psalms* (Ada, MI: Baker Publishing Group, 2012), chap. 63.

5. Charles Spurgeon, *The Treasury of David* (New York: Funk & Wagnalls Co., 1882), 141. Quoting John Angell James.

6. Hugh Black, *Friendship* (Hachette UK: Hodder & Stoughton, 1897), 195.

7. Bullock, Strauss, Walton, *Psalms Vol 1* (Ada, MI: Baker Publishing Group, 2015), 1183.

8. John Preston and James T. O'Brien, *The Fullness of Christ* (Simpsonville, SC: New Puritan Press, 2012), location 154, Kindle version.

9. Mark D. Futato, The Book of Psalms in *Cornerstone Biblical Commentary, vol 7: The Book of Psalms, The Book of Proverbs* (Carol Stream, IL: Tyndale House Publishers, 2009), 213.

10. Samuel Rutherford, LXXIX, Letters of Samuel Rutherford.

CHAPTER 6

1. Wisdom 7:10, GNT.

2. Bruce K. Waltke, *The Book of Proverbs, Chapters 1–15* (Grand Rapids, MI: Eerdmans Publishing Company, 2004), 182.

3. Saint Augustine, *Answer to the Pelagians* (Hyde Park, NY: New City Press, 2003),140.

4. Anne Stewart, *Poetic Ethics in Proverbs* (Cambridge, England: Cambridge University Press, 2016), 85-86.

5. John Calvin, *The Institutes of the Christian Religion*, I.1.i.

6. Tremper Longman, *Proverbs, Baker Commentary on the Old Testament Wisdom and Psalms* (Ada, MI: Baker Publishing Group, 2006), 137.

7. Wisdom 8:2,9,18

8. https://biblehub.com/commentaries/poole/proverbs/7.htm

9. Stewart, *Poetic Ethics in Proverbs,* 86.

10. Waltke, *The Book of Proverbs,* 194-95.

CHAPTER 7

1. Thomas Keneally, *Three Famines: Starvation and Politics* (Poland: Public Affairs, 2011), 53-54.

2. A.M. Wilson, *Wines of the Bible* (London, UK: Hamilton, Adams, and Co., 1877), 294.

3. J. Alec Motyer, *Isaiah: Tyndale Old Testament Commentary* (Nottingham: InterVarsity Press, 2009), 92.

CHAPTER 8

1. Tremper Longman and Raymond B. Dillard, *An Introduction to the Old Testament* (Grand Rapids, MI: Zondervan, 2006), 204.

2. Tremper Longman, *Daniel Commentary* (Grand Rapids, MI: Zondervan, 2011), 248.

3. David Frye, *Walls: A History of Civilization in Blood and Brick* (New York, NY: Scribner, 2019), 11.

4. Ibid.

5. Ibid., 7.

6. Mervin Breneman, *Ezra, Nehemiah, Esther, vol. 10* (Nashville, TN: Broadman & Holman Publishers, 1993), 224.

7. Peter Wohlleben, *The Hidden Life of Trees* (Vancouver: Greystone Books, 2015), 15-17.

8. Derek Kidner, *Ezra and Nehemiah* (Downers Grove, IL: InterVarsity Press, 2016), 118.

9. See Deuteronomy 30:34; Nehemiah 1:8-9; Isaiah 40:11; 43:5; 54:7; 56:8; Jeremiah 23:3; 29:14; 31:8,10; 32:37; Ezekiel 11:17; 20:34,41; 28:25; 34:13; 36:24; 37:21; 39:27; Micah 2:12; 4:6.

10. Kidner, *Ezra and Nehemiah,*126.

11. See Hosea 6:6; Isaiah 29:13; 58:2.

12. Gordon Fay Davies, *Ezra and Nehemiah* (Collegeville, MN: Liturgical Press, 1999), 112.

CHAPTER 9

1. Plutarch, *Table Talk*, https://web.archive.org/web/20190902071013/https ://ebooks.adelaide.edu.au/p/plutarch/symposiacs/chapter1.html.

2. Luke 1:52-53

3. Darrell L. Bock, *A Theology of Luke and Acts* (Grand Rapids, MI: Zondervan, 2012), 355.

4. See Luke 6:20,21; 11:41; 12:33; 14:12-24; 18:14, 22, 24.

5. Dennis E. Smith, *From Symposium to Eucharist: The Banquet in the Early Christian World* (Minneapolis, MN: Augsburg Fortress, 2003), 269.

6. Jeannine K. Brown, *The Gospels as Stories: A Narrative Approach to Matthew, Mark, Luke, and John* (Grand Rapids, MI: Baker Academic, 2020), 57.

7. In Luke 6:1, Jesus' disciples pluck heads of grain on the Sabbath and in 6:6, he heals a man with a withered hand.

8. Joel B. Green, *The Gospel of Luke* (United Kingdom: Eerdmans Publishing Company, 1997), 5.5.4.

9. Jerome H. Neyrey, "Loss of Wealth, Loss of Family and Loss of Honour: The cultural context of the original makarisms in Q" in *Modelling Early Christianity: Social-Scientific Studies of the New Testament in Its Context*, ed. Philip Esler (New York: Routledge, 2002), 136.

10. Smith, *From Symposium to Eucharist*, 253.

11. Joel C. Relihan, "Rethinking the History of the Literary Symposium," *Illinois Classical Studies* 17, no. 2 (1992): 218, www.jstor.org/stable/23064322.

12. https://archive.org/stream/moraliainfifteen08plutuoft/ moraliainfifteen08plutuoft_djvu.txt

13. Smith, *From Symposium to Eucharist*, 256.

14. Craig L. Blomberg, *Interpreting the Parables* (Downers Grove, IL: InterVarsity Press, 2012), 306.

15. Luke Timothy Johnson, *Sacra Pagina: The Gospel of Luke* (Minneapolis: Liturgical Press, 1991), 224.

16. Green, *The Gospel of Luke*, 5.5.4.2.

17. Ibid.

18. Plutarch, *On Love of Wealth*, 523C.

19. There are two Greek words for poor. One has the meaning of not able to afford anything extra, the second, which is used throughout Luke has the meaning of beggarly

20. Louise A. Gosbell, "Banqueting and Disability in the Ancient World: Reconsidering the Parable of the Great Banquet (Luke 14:15-24)" in *Theology*

and the Experience of Disability, ed. Andrew Pickard and Myk Habets, 129-144. (United Kingdom: Routledge, 2016), 135.

21. 1 QSa 2:3-9, The Rule of the Congregation

22. Gosbell, "Banqueting and Disability in the Ancient World," 140.

23. Ibid.

24. John Nolland, *Luke 9:21–18:34, volume 35B* (Grand Rapids: Zondervan, 1993), 751.

25. Mikeal Carl Parsons, *The Bible and Disability: A Commentary* (Waco: Baylor University Press, 2017), 304.

26. Gosbell, "Banqueting and Disability in the Ancient World," 144.

27. Candida R. Moss, "Mark and Matthew" in *The Bible and Disability: A Commentary*, eds. Sarah J. Melcher, Mikeal C. Parsons, and Amos Yong (Waco TX: Baylor Univ. Press, 2017), 330.

28. Craig Blomberg, *Contagious Holiness: Jesus' Meals with Sinners* (Downers Grove, IL: InterVarsity Press, 2005), 148. Micah 4:6 says, "In that day, I will assemble the lame."

CHAPTER 10

1. Craig L. Blomberg, *Jesus and the Gospels* (Nashville, TN: B&H Publishing Group, 2009), 164.

2. Herman N. Ridderbos, The *Coming of the Kingdom* (Philadelphia, PA: P&R Publishing Company, 1962), 152.

3. Blomberg, *Interpreting the Parables,* 215-16. There's a rabbinic version, the Gospel of Thomas version and a gnostic gospel of truth version.

4. Ridderbos, *The Coming of the Kingdom,* 235.

5. Randolph E. Richards, *Misreading Scripture with Individualist Eyes* (Downers Grove, IL: InterVarsity Press, 2020), 235.

6. Luke Timothy Johnson, *Sacra Pagina,* in the Mishnah, 237.

7. Dane Ortlund, *Gentle and Lowly* (Wheaton, IL: Crossway, 2020), 19.

8. Bock, *Luke,* 1315.

9. Alexander MacLaren, *MacLaren's Commentary: Expositions of Holy Scripture* (Fort Collins, CO: Delmarva Publications, Inc., n.d.), n.p. https://www .google.com/books/edition/MacLaren_s_Commentary_Expositions_of_Hol /YkPwCQAAQBAJ?hl=en&gbpv=1.

10. Ibid.

11. C.S. Lewis, *Mere Christianity* (San Francisco, CA: HarperOne, 2009), 122.

12. Bock, *Luke,* 1319.

13. Edward Welch, *Shame Interrupted: How God Lifts the Pain of Worthlessness and Rejection* (Greensboro, NC: New Growth Press, 2012), 62.

14. John Preston and James T. O'Brien, *The Fullness of Christ* (Simpsonville, SC: New Puritan Press, 2012), location 194, Kindle version.

15. Amy Carmichael, *If* (Fort Washington, PA: CLC Publications, 1992), 28.

16. Michael Ovey, *The Feasts of Repentance* (Downers Grove, IL: InterVarsity Press, 2019), 72.

17. MacLaren, *MacLaren's Commentary*, n.p..

CHAPTER 11

1. Thomas à Kempis, *The Imitation of Christ* (Chicago, IL: Moody Press, 1980), 317-18.

2. Charles C. Ellicott, *Ellicott's Commentary on the Whole Bible, vol. V, Jeremiah - Malachi* (Eugene, OR: Wipf & Stock, 2015), 231.

3. Richard B. Hays, *First Corinthians: Interpretation: A Bible Commentary for Teaching and Preaching* (Louisville, KY: Westminster John Knox Press, 2011), 193-94.

4. Ronald P. Hesselgrave, *The Supper: New Creation, Hospitality, and Hope in Christ* (Eugene, OR: Wipf & Stock, 2019), 112.

5. Hays, *First Corinthians*, 195.

6. Hesselgrave, *The Supper*, 112.

7. Ibid.

8. J. Todd Billings, *Remembrance, Communion, and Hope* (Grand Rapids, MI: Eerdmans Publishing Company, 2018), Kindle edition, chap. 3.

9. Ibid, chap. 1.

10. N. T. Wright, *The Meal Jesus Gave Us* (Louisville, KY: Presbyterian Publishing Corporation, 2002), 51.

11. Billings, *Remembrance*, Kindle edition, chap. 1.

CHAPTER 12

1. Dennis E. Johnson, *Triumph of the Lamb: A Commentary on Revelation* (Phillipsburg, NJ: P&R Publishing, 2001), 143.

2. Charles J. Ellicott, *Ellicott's Commentary on the Whole Bible, vol. VIII* (Eugene, OR: Wipf & Stock Publishers, 2015), 545.

3. Johnson, *Triumph of the Lamb*, 289-91.

4. Genesis 24:53; Exodus 22:15-16; Hosea 3:2.

5. C.H. Spurgeon, *Spurgeon's Sermons, vol. 02* (Ontario: Devoted Publishing, 2017), 6.

6. William Hendriksen, *More Than Conquerors* (Ada, MI: Baker Book Group, 1940), 92.

BIBLIOGRAPHY

1 QSa 2:3-9, The Rule of the Congregation.

à Kempis, Thomas. *The Imitation of Christ.* Chicago, IL: Moody Press, 1980.

Alexander, T. Desmond. *From Paradise to Promised Land.* Grand Rapids, MI: Baker Academic, 2012.

Allen, John S. *The Omnivorous Brain.* Cambridge, MA: Harvard University Press, 2012.

Augustine. *Answer to the Pelagians.* Hyde Park, NY: New City Press, 2003.

Baker, David Weston, Dale A. Brueggemann, Philip Wesley Comfort, Eugene H. Merril. *Leviticus, Numbers, Deuteronomy Vol. 2.* Carol Stream, IL: Tyndale House Publishers, 1996.

Barrs, Jerram. *Delighting in the Law of the Lord: God's Alternative to Legalism and Moralism.* Wheaton, IL: Crossway, 2013.

Billings, J. Todd. *Remembrance, Communion, and Hope.* Grand Rapids, MI: Eerdmans Publishing Company, 2018.

Black, Hugh. *Friendship.* Hachette, UK: Hodder & Stoughton, 1897.

Blomberg, Craig L. *Jesus and the Gospels.* Nashville, TN: B&H Publishing Group, 2009.

———. *Interpreting the Parables.* Downers Grove, IL: InterVarsity Press, 2012.

———. *Contagious Holiness: Jesus' Meals with Sinners.* Nottingham, UK: Apollos, 2005.

Bock, Darrell L. *A Theology of Luke and Acts.* Grand Rapids, MI: Zondervan, 2012.

———. *Luke.* Ada, MI: Baker Publishing, 1996.

Booker, Richard. *Celebrating Jesus in the Biblical Feasts.* Shippensburg, PA: Destiny Image Publishers, 2016.

Braun, Willi. *Feasting and Social Rhetoric in Luke 14.* United Kingdom: Cambridge University Press, 1995.

Breneman, M. *Ezra, Nehemiah, Esther Vol. 10.* Nashville, TN: Broadman & Holman Publishers, 1993.

Brown, D., A. R. Fausset, & R. Jamieson. *A Commentary, Critical, Experimental, and Practical, on the Old and New Testaments: Genesis–Deuteronomy Vol. I.* London; Glasgow, UK: William Collins, Sons, & Company, Limited, n.d.

Brown, Jeannine K. *The Gospels as Stories.* Grand Rapids, MI: Baker Academic, 2020.

Broyles, Craig C. *Psalms.* Ada, MI: Baker Publishing Group, 2012.

Bruckner, James K. *Exodus Commentary.* Peabody, MA: Hendrickson Publishers, 2008.

Buechner, Frederick. *A Room Called Remember.* San Francisco, CA: HarperOne, 2009.

———. *Secrets in the Dark.* San Francisco, CA: HarperOne, 2009.

Bullock, Strauss Walton. *Psalms Vol 1.* Ada, MI: Baker Publishing Group, 2015.

Caird, George. *The Exegetical Method of the Epistle to the Hebrews.* Canadian Journal of Theology 5 (1959).

Calvin, John. *The Institutes of Christian Religion.*

Carmichael, Amy. *If.* Fort Washington, PA: CLC Publications, 1992.

Davies, Gordon Fay. *Ezra and Nehemiah.* Collegeville, MN: Liturgical Press, 1999.

deClaisse-Walford, Nancy L., Rolf A. Jacobson, and Beth LaNeel Tanner. *The Book of Psalms: The New International Commentary on the Old Testament.* Grand Rapids, MI: Eerdmans Publishing Company, 2014.

Duguid, Iain M. *Numbers: God's Presence in the Wilderness.* Wheaton, IL: Crossway, 2012.

Ellicott, Charles C. *Ellicott's Commentary on the Whole Bible Volume V Jeremiah – Malachi.* Eugene, OR: Wipf & Stock, 2015.

Erdman, Charles R. *The Book of Leviticus: An Exposition.* Grand Rapids, MI: Baker Book House, 1951.

Frye, David. *Walls: A History of Civilization in Blood and Brick.* New York, NY: Scribner, 2019.

Futato, M. D. *The Book of Psalms. Cornerstone Biblical Commentary, Vol 7:*

The Book of Psalms, The Book of Proverbs. Carol Stream, IL: Tyndale House Publishers, 2009.

Goldingay, John. *Psalms: Psalms 1-41*. Ada, MI: Baker Publishing Group, 2006.

———. *Psalms: Psalms 42-89*. Ada, MI: Baker Publishing Group, 2007.

Gosbell, Louise A. "Banqueting and Disability in the Ancient World: Reconsidering the Parable of the Great Banquet (Luke 14:15-24)" in *Theology and the Experience of Disability*, ed. Andrew Pickard and Myk Habets, 129-144. United Kingdom: Routledge, 2016.

Green, Joel B. *The Gospel of Luke*. Grand Rapids, MI: Eerdmans Publishing Company, 1997.

Greenberg, Irving. *The Jewish Way: Living the Jewish Holidays*. New York, NY: Touchstone, 2011.

Hays, Richard B. *Echoes of Scripture in the Gospels*. Waco, TX: Baylor University Press, 2016.

———. *First Corinthians: Interpretation: A Bible Commentary for Teaching and Preaching*. Louisville, KY: Westminster John Knox Press, 2011.

Hendriksen, William. *More Than Conquerors*. Ada, MI: Baker Book Group, 1940.

Hesselgrave, Ronald P. *The Supper: New Creation, Hospitality, and Hope in Christ*. Eugene, OR: Wipf & Stock, 2019.

Huffstetler, Joel W. *Boundless Love: The Parable of the Prodigal Son and Reconciliation*. Lanham, MD: University Press of America, 2008.

Isaacs, Ronald H. *Every Person's Guide to Shavuot*. Lanham, MD: Jason Aronson, 1999.

Jerome H. Neyrey, "Loss of Wealth, Loss of Family and Loss of Honour: The Cultural Context of the Original Makarisms in Q" in *Modelling Early Christianity: Social-Scientific Studies of the New Testament in Its Context*, ed. Philip Esler. New York, NY: Routledge, 2002.

Johnson, Dennis E. *Triumph of the Lamb: A Commentary on Revelation*. Phillipsburg, NJ: P&R Publishing, 2001.

Johnson, Luke Timothy. *Sacra Pagina: The Gospel of Luke*. Minneapolis, MN: Liturgical Press, 1991.

Keneally, Thomas. *Three Famines: Starvation and Politics*. Poland: Public Affairs, 2011.

Kidner, Derek, *Ezra and Nehemiah*. Downers Grove, IL: InterVarsity Press, 2016.

———. *Psalms 1-72*. Downers Grove, IL: InterVarsity Press, 2014.

Ko, Ming Him. *Leviticus: A Pastoral and Contextual Commentary*. Carlisle, UK: Langham Creative Projects, 2018.

Lees, Frederick Richard and James Dawson Burns. *Temperance Bible Commentary*. London, UK: S. W. Partridge, 1868.

Lewis, C. S. *Mere Christianity*. San Francisco, CA: HarperOne, 2009.

Liefeld, Walter L. and David W. Pao. *Luke: The Expositor's Bible Commentary*. Grand Rapids, MI: Zondervan Academic, 2009.

Longenecker, Richard N. *Acts: The Expositor's Bible Commentary*. Grand Rapids, MI: Zondervan Academic, 2017.

Longman, Tremper and Raymond B. Dillard. *An Introduction to the Old Testament*. Grand Rapids, MI: Zondervan, 2006.

———. *Daniel Commentary*. Grand Rapids, MI: Zondervan, 2011.

———. *Proverbs: Baker Commentary on the Old Testament Wisdom and Psalms*. Ada, MI: Baker Publishing Group, n.d.

Lundbom, Jack R. *Deuteronomy: A Commentary*. Grand Rapids, MI: Eerdmans Publishing Company, 2013.

MacIntyre, Alasdair. *After Virtue: A Study in Moral Theory*. United Kingdom: Bloomsbury Publishing, 2013.

MacLaren, Alexander. *MacLaren's Commentary: Expositions of Holy Scripture*. Fort Collins, CO: Delmarva Publications, Inc., n.d.

Marshall, I. Howard. *Acts: An Introduction and Commentary*. Nottingham, UK: InterVarsity Press, 2008.

Morris, Leon. *The Atonement: Its Meaning & Significance*. Downers Grove, IL: InterVarsity Press, 1983.

Moss, Candida R. "Mark and Matthew" in *The Bible and Disability: A Commentary*, eds. Sarah J. Melcher, Mikeal C. Parsons, and Amos Yong. Waco, TX: Baylor Univ. Press, 2017.

Motyer, J. Alec. *Isaiah: Tyndale Old Testament Commentary*. Nottingham, UK: InterVarsity Press, 2009.

———. *The Message of Exodus: The Days of Our Pilgrimage*. Downers Grove, IL: InterVarsity Press, 2005.

Nolland, John. *Luke 9:21-18:34, Volume 35B*. Grand Rapids, MI: Zondervan, 1993.

Ortlund, Dane. *Gentle and Lowly: The Heart of Christ for Sinners and Sufferers*. Wheaton, IL: Crossway, 2020.

Ovey, Michael J. *The Feasts of Repentance*. Downers Grove, IL: InterVarsity Press, 2019.

Parsons, Mikeal C. *Acts (Paideia: Commentaries on the New Testament)*. Grand Rapids, MI: Baker Academic, 2008.

———. *The Bible and Disability: A Commentary*. Waco, TX: Baylor University Press, 2017.

Plutarch, *On Love of Wealth*.

———. *Table Talk*.

Preston, John, ed. James T. O'Brien. *The Fullness of Christ*. Simpsonville, SC: New Puritan Press, 2012.

Relihan, Joel C. "Rethinking the History of the Literary Symposium," *Illinois Classical Studies* 17, no. 2 (1992).

Richards, Randolph E. and Richard James. *Misreading Scripture with Individualist Eyes*. Downers Grove, IL: InterVarsity Press, 2020.

Ridderbos, H. *The Coming of the Kingdom*. Philadelphia, PA: P&R Publishing Company, 1962.

Roberts, Vaughan. *True Friendship*. Leyland, England: 10Publishing, 2013.

Rooker, M. F. *Leviticus Vol. 3A*. Nashville, TN: Broadman & Holman Publishers, 2000.

Rutherford, Samuel. *Letters of Samuel Rutherford*, LXXIX.

Ryken, Philip. *Exodus: Saved for God's Glory*. Wheaton, IL: Crossway, 2005.

Sklar, Jay. *Leviticus: An Introduction and Commentary*. Downers Grove, IL: InterVarsity Press Academic, 2013.

Smith, Dennis E. *From Symposium to Eucharist: The Banquet in the Early Christian World*. Minneapolis, MN: Augsburg Fortress, 2003.

Spurgeon, C. H. *Spurgeon's Sermons Volume 02*. Ingersoll, ON: Devoted Publishing, 2017.

———. *The Treasury of David*. New York, NY: Funk & Wagnalls Co., 1882.

Stewart, Anne. *Poetic Ethics in Proverbs*. Cambridge, UK: Cambridge University Press, 2016.

Waltke, Bruce K. *The Book of Proverbs 1-15*. Grand Rapids, MI: Eerdmans Publishing Company, 2004.

Waltke, B. K., J. M. Houston, & E. Moore. *The Psalms as Christian Worship: A Historical Commentary*. Grand Rapids, MI; Eerdmans Publishing Company, 2010.

Welch, Edward. *Shame Interrupted: How God Lifts the Pain of Worthlessness and Rejection*. Greensboro, NC: New Growth Press, 2012.

Wenham, Gordon J. *The Book of Leviticus*. Grand Rapids, MI: Eerdmans Publishing Company, 1994.

Wilson, A. M. *Wines of the Bible*. London, UK: Hamilton, Adams, and Co., 1877.

Wilson, Gerald H. *Psalms Vol. 1*. Grand Rapids, MI: Zondervan, 2014.

Wohlleben, Peter. *The Hidden Life of Trees*. Vancouver, BC: Greystone Books, 2015.

Wright, N. T. *The Meal Jesus Gave Us*. Louisville, KY: Presbyterian Publishing Corporation, 2002.

Bible Translations Used

Unless otherwise indicated, all Scripture quotations are taken from The ESV® Bible (The Holy Bible, English Standard Version®), copyright © 2001 by Crossway, a publishing ministry of Good News Publishers. Used by permission. All rights reserved.

Verses marked NIV are taken from the Holy Bible, New International Version®, NIV®. Copyright © 1973, 1978, 1984, 2011 by Biblica, Inc.® Used by permission of Zondervan. All rights reserved worldwide. www.zondervan.com. The "NIV" and "New International Version" are trademarks registered in the United States Patent and Trademark Office by Biblica, Inc.™

Verses marked NLT are taken from the Holy Bible, New Living Translation, copyright © 1996, 2004, 2015 by Tyndale House Foundation. Used by permission of Tyndale House Publishers, Inc., Carol Stream, Illinois 60188. All rights reserved.

Verses marked CEV are taken from the Contemporary English Version © 1991, 1992, 1995 by American Bible Society. Used by permission.

Verses marked NASB are taken from the (NASB®) New American Standard Bible®, Copyright © 1960, 1971, 1977, 1995, 2020 by The Lockman Foundation. Used by permission. All rights reserved. www.lockman.org.

Verses marked HCSB have been taken from the Holman Christian Standard Bible®, Copyright © 1999, 2000, 2002, 2003, 2009 by Holman Bible Publishers. Used by permission. Holman Christian Standard Bible®, Holman CSB®, and HCSB® are federally registered trademarks of Holman Bible Publishers.

Verses marked NRSV are taken from the New Revised Standard Version Bible, copyright © 1989 National Council of the Churches of Christ in the United States of America. Used by permission. All rights reserved worldwide.

Verses marked KJV are taken from the King James Version of the Bible.

ACKNOWLEDGMENTS

A few years out of college, after I moved back to the US after living in Asia, my dad told me I had a book in me and I laughed, I suppose like maybe Sarah laughed when she learned she'd have a child. Turns out we were both needlessly skeptical: a child came out of her and, alas, a book has come out of me. Soli Deo Gloria.

Several friends thought of me as a writer long before I ever saw myself that way, and I'm grateful for their constant support and encouragement: Stella Miji Byunn, who complimented all my emails, Justin Lancy, Hudson Hollister, Tree Girolamo, Michelle Witte, Rick Barry, and Letitia Harmon. You guys saw this coming way before I did.

Then there's the co-captains of the cheer squad, my two lovely housemates, book shower hosts Traci Emerson Spackey and Ashley Nelle-Davis. The prayers, patience, and thoughtfulness you've extended to me throughout this process and the many times I was excited for myself vicariously through you buoyed me. The other members of the cheer squad have shared in my joy in special ways: Kara Akins, Alyssa Kroboth, Rebekah Schmerber, Jay Bethard, Anna Laura Grant, Mazaré Rogers, Kelly Sampson, Leslie Mosteller, Juliet Vedral, Mike Wolf, Lisa McKay, Ruth Chan, Mary and Sam An, and Christina Eickenroht.

While I'm sure everyone thinks they have the best writing group, I really do. Thank you to the women of Grammatical Foibles who've provided feedback on my writing, answered countless questions I've had about the publishing process, and been there for me (and each other) in ways that, I suspect, go beyond what average writing groups do. I'm especially grateful to Courtney Ellis and Anna Woofenden for being like mentors and big sisters—at least writing-wise—to me, and for their friendship. Special thanks also to Bethany Rydmark, Rebecca Peet, and Lyndsey Medford who have provided feedback on drafts. I have grown tremendously as a writer in community with you.

I never knew you could love a librarian so much until I got to work with the RTS-DC librarian, Kimberley Stephenson. She was able to quickly locate the most obscure of articles and book chapters used in my research. Trying to access books during a pandemic when you're homebound wasn't the nightmare I thought it would be.

The pastoral staff and teaching elders at my church have enthusiastically encouraged the use of my gifts, prayed for my writing ministry, and made the dream of seminary possible.

Thank you to my wonderful professors at RTS whose influence I see on the pages of this book, Scott Redd, Tommy Keene, and Peter Lee. I have been blessed by your humility, instruction, and encouragement. Without Professor Redd's support, I also would not have met my literary agent, Brad Byrd, whose support, advocacy, and enthusiasm has been a boon throughout this whole process.

To my chapter editors, you guys were amazing to work with. Thank you for making this book better. And to my beta readers Meg Montee, Will Stockdale, and Adjwoa Acheamphong, I am truly in your debt. Last but not least on the editing front, thank you Kathleen Kerr for believing in my voice and in this project.

Finally, to my family—especially my mother, Sharon Akins, who has always been proud of me and supported my efforts: thank you for always reminding me I can do more than I think.

About the Author

Alicia J. Akins is a writer and recovering expat based in DC. After living and working in Asia for five years, she considers it a second home. She is a Master of Arts in Biblical Studies student at RTS, Washington, and serves as a deaconess in her church, Grace DC Downtown. You can find more of her writing at FeetCryMercy.com and follow her on Twitter @feetcrymercy.